EXPERIENCE

Trauma, Narrative, and History

THE JOHNS HOPKINS UNIVERSITY PRESS BALTIMORE AND LONDON

© 1996 The Johns Hopkins University Press
All rights reserved. Published 1996
Printed in the United States of America on acid-free paper
9 8 7 6 5 4 3 2

The Johns Hopkins University Press
2715 North Charles Street
Baltimore, Maryland 21218-4363
www.press.jhu.edu

Library of Congress Cataloging-in-Publication Data
will be found at the end of this book.

A catalog record for this book is available from the British Library.

ISBN 0-8018-5246-3
ISBN 0-8018-5247-1 (pbk.)

To the students of "Literature, Trauma, and Culture"

CONTENTS

ACKNOWLEDGMENTS

I am grateful to Shoshana Felman for her inspiring work on testimony, for her astute listening, and for her deeply resonant responses to my writing. I would like to thank Geoffrey Hartman for a rich and complex dialogue on history and representation. Dori Laub, M.D., first introduced me to the world of contemporary trauma studies and has provided an ongoing dialogue on clinical trauma research. Cynthia Chase has been a crucial interlocutor in my thinking about trauma, and Jill Robbins has provided central insights into the relation between trauma and ethical thought. I am also grateful to Kevin Newmark for his excellent and thoughtful responses. Tom Greene has been a longtime interlocutor and has helped me to consider the literary dimensions of my study. And Harold Bloom has continued to provide a lively exchange on psychoanalysis and literature.

Others who have contributed with insight and careful judgment are Dolora Wojciehowski, Thomas Keenan, Thomas McCall, David Guenther, Lynn Enterline, Susan Nathiel, and my parents, who offered important insights concerning psychoanalytic theory. My former students Marjorie Allard, Michael Jasny, and Robert Hughes provided excellent and enthusiastic research. I would like, in addition, to thank each of my students in the different versions of "Literature, Trauma, and Culture," who meant so much to me during the writing of this book and who added immeasurably to the thinking that went into it. In the last stages, Joanne Allen did a meticulous job of copyediting, and Carol Zimmerman offered careful help with the proofs. Finally, I am grateful to Elizabeth Rottenberg for her engaged listening and for her crucial interventions.

Earlier versions of several chapters of this book have previously been published: chapter 1 in *Yale French Studies* 79, "Literature and the Ethical Question," ed. Claire Nouvet (winter 1991); chapter 4 in the *Yale Journal of Criticism*, October 1990, and reprinted in *Critical Encounters: Reference and Responsibility in Deconstructive Writing*, ed. Cathy Caruth and Deborah Esch (New Brunswick: Rutgers University Press, 1995); and a shorter version of chapter 5 in *Performativity and Performance*, Essays from the English Institute, ed. Andrew Parker and Eve Sedgwick (New York: Routledge, 1995).

UNCLAIMED EXPERIENCE

INTRODUCTION: THE WOUND AND THE VOICE

Though chilled with horror,
with a second blow
He struck it, and decided then to look.

Torquato Tasso, *Jerusalem Liberated*

In the third chapter of *Beyond the Pleasure Principle*, Freud describes a pattern of suffering that is inexplicably persistent in the lives of certain individuals. Perplexed by the terrifyingly literal nightmares of battlefield survivors and the repetitive reenactments of people who have experienced painful events, Freud wonders at the peculiar and sometimes uncanny way in which catastrophic events seem to repeat themselves for those who have passed through them. In some cases, Freud points out,

these repetitions are particularly striking because they seem not
to be initiated by the individual's own acts but rather appear as
the possession of some people by a sort of fate, a series of painful events to which they are subjected, and which seem to be
entirely outside their wish or control. "The most moving poetic
picture of a fate such as this," Freud writes, "can be found in the
story told by Tasso in his romantic epic *Gerusalemme Liberata*":

> Its hero, Tancred, unwittingly kills his beloved Clorinda in a
> duel while she is disguised in the armour of an enemy knight.
> After her burial he makes his way into a strange magic forest
> which strikes the Crusaders' army with terror. He slashes with
> his sword at a tall tree; but blood streams from the cut and the
> voice of Clorinda, whose soul is imprisoned in the tree, is heard
> complaining that he has wounded his beloved once again.[1]

The actions of Tancred, wounding his beloved in a battle and
then, unknowingly, seemingly by chance, wounding her again,
evocatively represent in Freud's text the way that the experience
of a trauma repeats itself, exactly and unremittingly, through
the unknowing acts of the survivor and against his very will. As
Tasso's story dramatizes it, the repetition at the heart of catastrophe—the experience that Freud will call "traumatic neurosis"—emerges as the unwitting reenactment of an event that
one cannot simply leave behind.

I would like to suggest here, however, that the literary resonance of Freud's example goes beyond this dramatic illustration
of repetition compulsion and exceeds, perhaps, the limits of
Freud's conceptual or conscious theory of trauma. For what
seems to me particularly striking in the example of Tasso is not
just the unconscious act of the infliction of the injury and its
inadvertent and unwished-for repetition, but the moving and
sorrowful *voice* that cries out, a voice that is paradoxically released *through the wound*. Tancred does not only repeat his act
but, in repeating it, he for the first time hears a voice that cries

out to him to see what he has done. The voice of his beloved addresses him and, in this address, bears witness to the past he has unwittingly repeated. Tancred's story thus represents traumatic experience not only as the enigma of a human agent's repeated and unknowing acts but also as the enigma of the otherness of a human voice that cries out from the wound, a voice that witnesses a truth that Tancred himself cannot fully know.

It is the moving quality of this literary story, I would suggest—its striking juxtaposition of the unknowing, injurious repetition and the witness of the crying voice—that best represents Freud's intuition of, and his passionate fascination with, traumatic experiences. If Freud turns to literature to describe traumatic experience, it is because literature, like psychoanalysis, is interested in the complex relation between knowing and not knowing. And it is at the specific point at which knowing and not knowing intersect that the language of literature and the psychoanalytic theory of traumatic experience precisely meet. The example offered by the poetry of Tasso is indeed, in my interpretation, more than a literary example of a vaster psychoanalytic, or experiential, truth; the poetic story can be read, I will suggest, as a larger parable, both of the unarticulated implications of the theory of trauma in Freud's writings and, beyond that, of the crucial link between literature and theory that the following pages set out to explore.

A DOUBLE WOUND

As the repeated infliction of a wound, the act of Tancred calls up the originary meaning of trauma itself (in both English and German), the Greek *trauma*, or "wound," originally referring to an injury inflicted on a body.[2] In its later usage, particularly in the medical and psychiatric literature, and most centrally in Freud's text, the term *trauma* is understood as a wound inflicted not upon the body but upon the mind. But what seems to be suggested by Freud in *Beyond the Pleasure Principle* is that the wound of the mind—the breach in the mind's experience of time, self, and the world—is not, like the wound of the body, a simple and healable event, but rather an event that, like Tancred's first infliction of a mortal wound on the disguised Clorinda in the duel, is experienced too soon, too unexpectedly, to be fully known and is therefore not available to consciousness until it imposes itself again, repeatedly, in the nightmares and repetitive actions of the survivor.[3] Just as Tancred does not hear the voice of Clorinda until the second wounding, so trauma is not locatable in the simple violent or original event in an individual's past, but rather in the way that its very unassimilated nature—the way it was precisely *not known* in the first instance—returns to haunt the survivor later on.[4]

What the parable of the wound and the voice thus tells us, and what is at the heart of Freud's writing on trauma, both in what it says and in the stories it unwittingly tells, is that trauma seems to be much more than a pathology, or the simple illness of a wounded psyche: it is always the story of a wound that cries out, that addresses us in the attempt to tell us of a reality or truth that is not otherwise available. This truth, in its delayed appearance and its belated address, cannot be linked only to what is known, but also to what remains unknown in our very actions and our language.

In this book I explore the ways in which texts of a certain period—the texts of psychoanalysis, of literature, and of literary theory—both speak about and speak through the profound story of traumatic experience. Rather than straightforwardly describing actual case studies of trauma survivors, or attempting to elucidate directly the psychiatry of trauma, the chapters that follow explore the complex ways that knowing and not knowing are entangled in the language of trauma and in the stories associated with it. Whether the texts I read concern, as in Freud, the theory of trauma in individual or collective history or, as in Duras and Resnais, the story of two people bonded in and around their respective catastrophic experiences, each one of these texts engages, in its own specific way, a central problem of listening, of knowing, and of representing that emerges from the actual experience of the crisis. If traumatic experience, as Freud indicates suggestively, is an experience that is not fully assimilated as it occurs, then these texts, each is in its turn, ask what it means to transmit and to theorize around a crisis that is marked, not by a simple knowledge, but by the ways it simultaneously defies and demands our witness. Such a question, I will argue, whether it occurs within a strictly literary text or in a more deliberately theoretical one, can never be asked in a straightforward way, but must, indeed, also be spoken in a language that is always somehow literary: a language that defies, even as it claims, our understanding.

In my own endeavor at interpretation, likewise, in the chapters on psychoanalytic writing and in the chapters on literature and literary theory, I attempt not just to follow each author's argument in its explicit reference to traumatic experience (Freud's theory of trauma as outlined in *Beyond the Pleasure Principle* and *Moses and Monotheism*, the notion of reference and the figure of the falling body in de Man, Kleist, and Kant, the mutual narratives of personal catastrophe in Duras and Resnais's *Hiroshima mon amour*, Lacan's rethinking of trauma in his interpretation of Freud's texts). My main endeavor is, rather, to trace in each of these texts a different story, the story or the textual itinerary of insistently recurring words or figures. The key figures my analysis uncovers and highlights—the figures of "departure," "falling," "burning," or "awakening"—in their insistence, here engender stories that in fact emerge out of the rhetorical potential and the literary resonance of these figures, a literary dimension that cannot be reduced to the thematic content of the text or to what the theory encodes, and that, beyond what we can know or theorize about it, stubbornly persists in bearing witness to some forgotten wound.

THE STORY OF AN ACCIDENT

At the heart of these stories is thus an enigmatic testimony not only to the nature of violent events but to what, in trauma, resists simple comprehension. And it is in way that we can also read one of the central lessons in Freud's recurrent attempts to grapple with the description and conceptualization of trauma. For what returns to haunt the trauma victim in Freud's primary example of trauma, as I emphasize in my readings of Freud's *Beyond the Pleasure Principle* and *Moses and Monotheism,* is not just any event but, significantly, the shocking and unexpected occurrence of an accident. The example of the train accident—the accident from which a person walks away apparently unharmed, only to suffer symptoms of the shock weeks later—most obviously illustrates, for Freud, the traumatizing shock of a commonly occurring violence. Yet the recurring image of the accident in Freud, as the illustration of the unexpected or the accidental, seems to be especially compelling, and indeed becomes the exemplary scene of trauma *par excellence,* not only because it depicts what we can know about traumatizing events, but also, and more profoundly, because it tells of what it is, in traumatic events, that is *not* precisely grasped. The accident, that is, as it emerges in Freud and is passed on through other trauma narratives, does not simply represent the violence of a collision but also conveys the impact of its very incomprehensibility. What returns to haunt the victim, these stories tell us, is not only the reality of the violent event but also the reality of the way that its violence has not yet been fully known.

The story of the accident thus refers us, indirectly, to the unexpected reality—the locus of referentiality—of the traumatic story. It is this link between narrative and reality that I explore in my chapter on Paul de Man's notion of referentiality, a notion that indeed associates reference with an impact, and specifically the impact of a fall. In my analysis of de Man's work, through his readings, in particular, of the philosophical texts of Immanuel Kant and the literary texts of Heinrich von Kleist, I attempt to show how de Man's critical theory of reference ultimately becomes a narrative, and a narrative inextricably bound up with the problem of what it means to fall (which is, perhaps, de Man's own translation of the concept—of the experience—of trauma). The story of the falling body—which I read through de Man's texts as the story of the impact of reference—thus encounters, unexpectedly, the story of a trauma, and the story of trauma is inescapably bound to a referential return.[5] This interpretation of reference through trauma, therefore, this understanding of trauma in terms of its indirect relation to reference, does not deny or eliminate the possibility of reference but insists, precisely, on the inescapability of its belated impact.[6]

TRAUMA AND HISTORY

The story of trauma, then, as the narrative of a belated experience, far from telling of an escape from reality—the escape from a death, or from its referential force—rather attests to its endless impact on a life. In Tasso's story, indeed, as we read it in Freud, Tancred does not escape the reality of death's impact—of the wounding accident and of Clorinda's death—but rather has to live it twice. The crisis at the core of many traumatic narratives—as I show concretely in my readings of Freud, Duras, and Lacan—often emerges, indeed, as an urgent question: Is the trauma the encounter with death, or the ongoing experience of having survived it? At the core of these stories, I would suggest, is thus a kind of double telling, the oscillation between a *crisis of death* and the correlative *crisis of life:* between the story of the unbearable nature of an event and the story of the unbearable nature of its survival. These two stories, both incompatible and absolutely inextricable, ultimately define the complexity of what I refer to as *history* in the texts that I read: in *Moses and Monotheism,* the intricate relation between the story of the Jews and the story of the Christians; in *Beyond the Plea-sure Principle*, the intertwining of the confrontation with death and the confrontation with life; in *Hiroshima mon amour* and in Lacan's interpretation of the dream of the burning child, the profound link between the death of the loved one and the ongoing life of the survivor. In these texts, as I suggest, it is the inextricability of the story of one's life from the story of a death, an impossible and necessary double telling, that constitutes their historical witness.[7]

THE VOICE OF THE OTHER

The theoretical and literary thrust of the present book can thus be illustrated in another way as well through Tasso's story—and through Freud's example—of the crying wound. For while the story of Tancred, the repeated thrusts of his unwitting sword and the suffering he recognizes through the voice he hears, represents the experience of an individual traumatized by his own past—the repetition of his own trauma as it shapes his life—the wound that speaks is not precisely Tancred's own but the wound, the trauma, of another. It is possible, of course, to understand that other voice, the voice of Clorinda, within the parable of the example, to represent the other within the self that retains the memory of the "unwitting" traumatic events of one's past. But we can also read the address of the voice here, not as the story of the individual in relation to the events of his own past, but as the story of the way in which one's own trauma is tied up with the trauma of another, the way in which trauma may lead, therefore, to the encounter with another, through the very possibility and surprise of listening to another's wound.

I would suggest that such a listening to the voice and to the speech delivered by the other's wound is what takes place, indeed, in Freud's own text, whose theory of trauma is written not only about but in the midst of trauma. The story of Tancred is thus equally, I would suggest, the story of psychoanalytic writing itself. The figure of Tancred addressed by the speaking wound constitutes, in other words, not only a parable of trauma and of its uncanny repetition but, more generally, a parable of psychoanalytic theory itself as it listens to a voice that it cannot fully know but to which it nonetheless bears witness.[8]

This listening to the address of another, an address that remains enigmatic yet demands a listening and a response, is what, in other ways, is also at the heart of the texts of Duras and of Lacan. In *Hiroshima mon amour* it is at the heart of the encounter between the woman and the man, between the French woman who has watched her German lover die in the war and the Japanese man whose family has been decimated by the bomb at Hiroshima and who turns out, profoundly and significantly, to be the only one able to hear and to receive, across the distance of their cultures and through the impact of their very different traumas, the woman's address. Likewise, this listening to another who addresses us forms the center of Lacan's reinterpretation of Freud's narrative of the dream of the burning child, through the emphasis it lays on the encounter between father and child: between a child who has died from a fever and whose corpse catches fire from an accidentally overturned candle; and a sleeping father, unconscious of this burning in the next room, who hears in his dream the voice of his dead child pleading for him to see the fire by whispering the words, "Father, don't you see I'm burning?" It is this plea by an other who is asking to be seen and heard, this call by which the other commands us to awaken (to awaken, indeed, to a burning), that resonates in different ways throughout the texts this book attempts to read, and which, in this book's understanding, constitutes the new mode of reading and of listening that both the language of trauma, and the silence of its mute repetition of suffering, profoundly and imperatively demand.

1 UNCLAIMED EXPERIENCE: TRAUMA AND THE POSSIBILITY OF HISTORY

(Freud, *Moses and Monotheism*)

It took the war to teach it, that you were as responsible for everything you saw as you were for everything you did. The problem was that you didn't always know what you were seeing until later, maybe years later, that a lot of it never made it in at all, it just stayed stored there in your eyes.

Michael Herr, *Dispatches*

Recent literary criticism has shown an increasing concern that the epistemological problems raised by poststructuralist criticism necessarily lead to political and ethical paralysis. The possibility that reference is indirect, and that consequently we may not have direct access to others', or even our own, histories, seems to imply the impossibility of access to other cultures and hence of any means of making political or ethical judgments.[1]

To such an argument I would like to contrast a phenomenon that not only arises in the reading of literary or philosophical texts but emerges most prominently within the wider historical and political realms, that is, the peculiar and paradoxical experience of trauma. In its most general definition, trauma describes an overwhelming experience of sudden or catastrophic events in which the response to the event occurs in the often delayed, uncontrolled repetitive appearance of hallucinations and other intrusive phenomena.² The experience of the soldier faced with sudden and massive death around him, for example, who suffers this sight in a numbed state, only to relive it later on in repeated nightmares, is a central and recurring image of trauma in our century. As a consequence of the increasing occurrence of such perplexing war experiences and other catastrophic responses during the last twenty years, physicians and psychiatrists have begun to reshape their thinking about physical and mental experience, including most recently the responses to a wide variety of other experiences, such as rape, child abuse, auto and industrial accidents, and so on, that are now often understood in terms of the effects of *post-traumatic stress disorder.* I would propose that it is here, in the equally widespread and bewildering encounter with trauma—both in its occurrence and in the attempt to understand it—that we can begin to recognize the possibility of a history that is no longer straightforwardly referential (that is, no longer based on simple models of experience and reference). Through the notion of trauma, I will argue, we can understand that a rethinking of reference is aimed not at eliminating history but at resituating it in our understanding, that is, at precisely permitting *history* to arise where *immediate understanding* may not.

The question of history is raised most urgently in one of the first works of trauma in this century, Sigmund Freud's history of the Jews entitled *Moses and Monotheism.* Because of its seeming fictionalization of the Jewish past, this work has raised ongoing questions about its historical and political status, yet its confrontation with trauma seems, nonetheless, to be deeply tied to our own historical realities. I have chosen this text as a focus of analysis, therefore, because I believe it can help us understand our own catastrophic era, as well as the difficulties of writing a history from within it. I will suggest that it is in the notion of history that Freud offers in this work, as well as in the way his writing itself confronts historical events, that we may need to rethink the possibility of history, as well as our ethical and political relation to it.

■ EXODUS, OR THE HISTORY OF A DEPARTURE

The entanglement of Freud's *Moses and Monotheism* with its own urgent historical context is evident in a letter written to Arnold Zweig in 1934, while Freud is working on the book, and while Nazi persecutions of the Jews are progressing at rapid speed. Freud says:

> Faced with the new persecutions, one asks oneself again how the Jews have come to be what they are and why they have attracted this undying hatred. I soon discovered the formula: Moses created the Jews.[3]

The project of *Moses and Monotheism* is clearly linked, in these lines, to the attempt to explain the Nazi persecution of the Jews. But this can apparently be done, according to Freud, only through reference to a past, and in particular to the past represented by Moses. By placing the weight of his history on the naming of Moses, moreover, the liberator of the Hebrews who led them out of Egypt, Freud implicitly and paradoxically connects the explanation of the Jews' persecution to their very liberation, the return from captivity to freedom. In the centrality of Moses thus lies the centrality of a return, the return of the Hebrews to Canaan, where they had lived prior to their settlement, and bondage, in Egypt. *Moses and Monotheism*'s most direct reference to, and explanation of, its present historical context will consist in Freud's new understanding of the story of captivity, or exile, and return.[4]

The notion of Jewish history as a history of return might seem unsurprising in the perspective of a psychoanalyst, whose works repeatedly focus on the necessity of various kinds of return—on the return to origins in memory and on the "return of the repressed." But in the description of his discovery, in the concise little formula jotted down for Zweig, "Moses created the Jews," Freud suggests that the history of the Jews surpasses any simple notion of return. For if Moses indeed "created" the Jews,[5] in his act of liberation—if the exodus from Egypt, that is, transforms the history of the *Hebrews*, who had previously lived in Canaan, into the history of the *Jews*, who become a true nation only in their act of leaving captivity—then the moment of beginning, the exodus from Egypt, is no longer simply a return but is rather, more truly, a departure. The question with which Freud frames his text, and which will explain both the Jews' historical situation and his own participation, as a Jewish writer, within it, is thus: In what way is the history of a culture, and its relation to a politics, inextricably bound up with the notion of departure?[6]

Freud's surprising account of Jewish history can be understood, indeed, as a reinterpretation of the nature, as well as the significance, of the Hebrews' return from captivity. In the biblical account, Moses was one of the captive Hebrews, who eventually arose as their leader and led them out of Egypt back to Canaan. Freud, on the other hand, announces at the beginning of his account that Moses, though the liberator of the Hebrew people, was not in fact himself a Hebrew, but an Egyptian, a fervent follower of an Egyptian pharaoh and his sun-centered monotheism. After the pharaoh's murder, according to Freud, Moses became a leader of the Hebrews and brought them out of Egypt in order to preserve the waning monotheistic religion.

Freud thus begins his story by changing the very reason for the return: it is no longer primarily the preservation of Hebrew freedom, but of the monotheistic god; that is, it is not so much the return to a freedom of the past as a departure into a newly established future—the future of monotheism.[7] In this rethinking of Jewish beginnings, then, the future is no longer continuous with the past but is united with it through a profound discontinuity. The exodus from Egypt, which shapes the meaning of the Jewish past, is a departure that is both a radical break and the establishment of a history.

The second part of Freud's account extends, and redoubles, this rethinking of the return. For after the Egyptian Moses led the Hebrews from Egypt, Freud claims, they murdered him in a rebellion; repressed the deed; and in the passing of two generations assimilated his god to a volcano god named Yahweh, and assimilated the liberating acts of Moses to the acts of another man, the priest of Yahweh (also named Moses), who was separated from the first in time and place. The most significant moment in Jewish history is thus, according to Freud, not the literal return to freedom, but the repression of a murder and its effects:

> The god Jahve attained undeserved honour when ... Moses' deed of liberation was put down to his account; but he had to pay dear for this usurpation. The shadow of the god whose place he had taken became stronger than himself; at the end of the historical development there arose beyond his being that of the forgotten Mosaic god. None can doubt that it was only the idea of this other god that enabled the people of Israel to surmount all their hardships and to survive until our time. (62; 50–51)[8]

If the return to freedom is the literal starting point of the history of the Jews, what constitutes the essence of their history is the repression, and return, of the deeds of Moses. The nature

of literal return is thus displaced by the nature of another kind
of reappearance:

> To the well-known *duality* of [Jewish] history . . . we add two
> new ones: the founding of *two* new religions, the first one ousted
> by the second and yet reappearing victorious, *two* founders of
> religion, who are both called by the same name, Moses, and
> whose personalities we have to separate from each other. And all
> these dualities are necessary consequences of the first: one sec-
> tion of the people passed through what may properly be termed
> a traumatic experience which the other was spared. (64–65; 52)

The captivity and return, while the beginning of the history of
the Jews, is precisely available to them only through the experience of a trauma. It is the trauma, the forgetting (and return) of
the deeds of Moses, that constitutes the link uniting the old
with the new god, the people that leave Egypt with the people
that ultimately make up the nation of the Jews. Centering his
story in the nature of the leaving, and returning, constituted by
trauma, Freud resituates the very possibility of history in the
nature of a traumatic departure. We might say, then, that the
central question, by which Freud finally inquires into the relation between history and its political outcome, is: What does it
mean, precisely, for history to be the history of a trauma?

For many readers, Freud's questioning of history—his dis-
placement of the story of a liberating return by the story of a
trauma—has seemed to be a tacit denial of history. By replacing factual history with the curious dynamics of trauma, Freud
would seem to have doubly denied the possibility of historical
reference: first, by himself actually replacing historical fact with
his own speculations, and second, by suggesting that historical
memory, or Jewish historical memory at least, is always a matter of distortion, a filtering of the original event through the fic-
tions of traumatic repression, which makes the event available

at best indirectly. Indeed, when Freud goes on, later in his work, to compare the Hebrews' traumatic experience to the traumas of the Oedipal boy, repressing his desire for the mother through the threat of castration, this leads many readers to assume that the only possible referential truth contained in Freud's text can be its own unconscious life, a kind of self-referential history that many have read as the story of Freud's "unresolved father complex."[9] And this analysis has itself reinterpreted the figure of departure and return in a very straightforward fashion, as Freud's departure from his father, or his departure from Judaism. For many critics the cost of Freud's apparently making history unconscious, or of his depriving history of its referential literality, is finally the fact that the text remains at best a predictable drama of Freud's unconscious, and, moreover, a drama that tells the story of political and cultural disengagement.[10]

THE TRAIN COLLISION, OR HISTORY AS ACCIDENT

When we attend closely, however, to Freud's own attempt to explain the trauma, we find a somewhat different understanding of what it means to leave and to return. While the analogy with the Oedipal individual constitutes much of his explanation, Freud opens this discussion with another example that is strangely unlikely as a comparison for a human history and yet resonates curiously with the particular history he has told. It is the example of an accident:

> It may happen that someone gets away, apparently unharmed, from the spot where he has suffered a shocking accident, for instance a train collision. In the course of the following weeks, however, he develops a series of grave psychical and motor symptoms, which can be ascribed only to his shock or whatever else happened at the time of the accident. He has developed a "traumatic neurosis." This appears quite incomprehensible and is therefore a novel fact. The time that elapsed between the accident and the first appearance of the symptoms is called the

"incubation period," a transparent allusion to the pathology of infectious disease. As an afterthought, it must strike us that—in spite of the fundamental difference in the two cases, the problem of the traumatic neurosis and that of Jewish monotheism—there is a correspondence in one point. It is the feature which one might term *latency*. There are the best grounds for thinking that in the history of the Jewish religion there is a long period, after the breaking away from the Moses religion, during which no trace is to be found of the monotheistic idea. . . . Thus . . . the solution of our problem is to be sought in a special psychological situation. (84; 67–68, translation modified)

In his use of the term *latency*, the period during which the effects of the experience are not apparent, Freud seems to compare the accident to the successive movement in Jewish history from the event to its repression to its return. Yet what is truly striking about the accident victim's experience of the event, and what in fact constitutes the central enigma revealed by Freud's example, is not so much the period of forgetting that occurs after the accident, but rather the fact that the victim of the crash was never fully conscious during the accident itself: the person gets away, Freud says, "apparently unharmed." The experience of trauma, the fact of latency, would thus seem to consist, not in the forgetting of a reality that can hence never be fully known, but in an inherent latency within the experience itself.[11] The historical power of the trauma is not just that the experience is repeated after its forgetting, but that it is only in and through its inherent forgetting that it is first experienced at all. And it is this inherent latency of the event that paradoxically explains the peculiar, temporal structure, the belatedness, of the Jews' historical experience: since the murder is not experienced as it occurs, it is fully evident only in connection with another place, and in another time. If return is displaced by trauma, then, this is significant insofar as its leaving—the space of unconsciousness—is, paradoxically, precisely what preserves the event in its literality. For history to be a history of trauma means that it is referential precisely to the extent that it is not fully perceived as it occurs; or to put it somewhat differently, that a history can be grasped only in the very inaccessibility of its occurrence.

The indirect referentiality of history is also, I would argue, at the core of Freud's understanding of the political shape of Jewish culture, in its repeated confrontation with anti-Semitism. For the murder of Moses, as Freud argues, is in fact a repetition of an earlier murder in the history of mankind, the murder of the primal father by his rebellious sons, which occurred in primeval history; and it is the unconscious repetition and acknowledgment of this fact that explains both Judaism and its Christian antagonists. Indeed, Freud says, when Paul interprets the death of Christ as the atonement for an original sin, he is belatedly and unconsciously remembering the murder of Moses, which still, in the history of the Jews, remains buried in unconsciousness. In belatedly atoning, as sons, for the father's murder, Christians feel Oedipal rivalry with their Jewish older brothers; a lingering castration anxiety, brought out by Jewish circumcision; and finally a complaint that the Jews will not admit the guilt that the Christians, in their recognition of Christ's death, have admitted. By appearing only belatedly, then, the historical effect of trauma, in Freud's text, is ultimately its inscription of the Jews in a history always bound to the history of the Christians. The Hebrews' departure, that is, or their arrival as a Jewish nation, is also an arrival within a history no longer simply their own. It is therefore, I would like to suggest, precisely in the very constitutive function of latency, in history, that Freud discovers the indissoluble, political bond to other histories. To put it somewhat differently, we could say that the traumatic nature of history means that events are only historical to the extent that they implicate others. And it is thus that Jewish history has also been the suffering of others' traumas.[12]

■ THE WRITING OF DISASTER

The full impact of this notion of history can only be grasped, however, when we turn to the question of what it would mean, in this context, to consider Freud's own writing as a historical act. In the various prefaces that he appends to his work, Freud himself imposes this question upon us by drawing our attention to the history of the text's own writing and publication. The actual writing of the book took place between 1934 and 1938, during the period of Freud's last years in Vienna, and his first year in London, to which he moved in June 1938 because of Nazi persecution of his family and of psychoanalysis. The first two parts of the book, containing the history of Moses, were published in 1937, before he left Austria, while the third part, containing the more extensive analysis of religion in general, was withheld from publication until 1938, after Freud had moved to London. In the middle of this third part Freud inserts what he calls a "Summary and Recapitulation" (or *Wiederholung*, literally "repetition"), in which he tells the story of his book in his own way:

> The following part of this essay [the second section of part 3] cannot be sent forth into the world without lengthy explanations and apologies. For it is no other than a faithful, often literal repetition of the first part. . . . Why have I not avoided it? The answer to this question is . . . rather hard to admit. I have not been able to efface the traces of the unusual way in which this book came to be written.
>
> In truth it has been written twice over. The first time was a few years ago in Vienna, where I did not believe in the possibility of publishing it. I decided to put it away, but it haunted me like an unlaid ghost, and I compromised by publishing two parts of the book. . . . Then in March 1938 came the unexpected German invasion. It forced me to leave my home, but it also freed me of the fear lest my publishing the book might cause psychoanalysis to be forbidden in a country where its practice was still

allowed. No sooner had I arrived in England than I found the temptation of making my withheld knowledge accessible to the world irresistible. . . . I could not make up my mind to relinquish the two former contributions altogether, and that is how the compromise came about of adding unaltered a whole piece of the first version to the second, a device which has the disadvantage of extensive repetition. (131–32; 103–4)

Reading this story Freud tells of his own work—of a history whose traces cannot be effaced, which haunts Freud like a ghost and finally emerges in several publications involving extensive repetition—it is difficult not to recognize the story of the Hebrews—of Moses's murder, its effacement, and its unconscious repetition. The book itself, Freud seems to be telling us, is the site of a trauma; a trauma that in this case, moreover, appears to be historically marked by the events that, Freud says, divide the book into two halves: first, the infiltration of Nazism into Austria, causing Freud to withhold or repress the third part, and then the invasion of Austria by Germany, causing Freud to leave, and ultimately to bring the third part to light. The structure and history of the book, in its traumatic form of repression and repetitive reappearance, thus mark it as the very bearer of a historical truth that is itself involved in the political entanglement of Jews and their persecutors.

But significantly, in spite of the temptation to lend an immediate referential meaning to Freud's trauma in the German invasion and Nazi persecution, it is not, in fact, precisely the *direct reference* to the German invasion that can be said to locate the actual trauma in Freud's passage. For the invasion is characterized, not in terms of its attendant persecution and threats, of which the Freud family did in fact have their share, but in terms of the somewhat different emphasis of a simple line: "It forced me to leave my home, but it also freed me" [(Sie) zwang mich, die Heimat zu verlassen, befreite mich aber].[13] The trauma in

Freud's text is first of all a trauma of leaving, the trauma of *ver-lassen*. Indeed, it is this word that actually ties this "Summary and Recapitulation" itself to the traumatic structuring of the book, in its implicit referral to two earlier prefaces, appended to the beginning of part 3. These two prefaces, subtitled "Before March 1938" (while Freud was still in Vienna) and "In June 1938" (after Freud had resettled in London), describe, respectively, his reasons for not publishing the book and his decision finally to let it come to light, announced as following in the second preface:

> The exceptionally great difficulties which have weighed on me during the composition of this essay dealing with Moses . . . are the reason why this third and final part comes to have two different prefaces which contradict—indeed, even cancel—each other. For in the short interval between writing the two prefaces the outer conditions of the author have radically changed. Formerly I lived under the protection of the Catholic Church and feared that by publishing the essay I should lose that protection. . . . Then, suddenly, the German invasion. . . . In the certainty of persecution . . . I left *[verliess ich]*, with many friends, the city which from early childhood, through seventy-eight years, had been a home to me. (69–70; 57)

The "interval" between the prefaces, which Freud explicitly notes, and which is also the literal space between "Before March 1938" and "In June 1938," also marks, implicitly, the space of a trauma, a trauma not simply *denoted* by the words "German invasion," but rather *borne* by the words *verliess ich*, "I left." Freud's writing preserves history precisely within this gap in his text; and within the words of his leaving, words that do not simply refer, but, through their repetition in the later "Summary and Recapitulation," convey the impact of a history precisely as what *cannot be grasped* about leaving.

FROM CAPTIVITY TO FREEDOM, OR FREUD'S EXODUS

Indeed, in Freud's own theoretical explanation of trauma, in the example of the accident, it is, finally, *the act of leaving* that constitutes its central and enigmatic core:

> It may happen that someone gets away [*die Städte verlässt*, literally, "leaves the site"], apparently unharmed, from the spot where he has suffered a shocking accident, for instance a train collision.

The trauma of the accident, its very unconsciousness, is borne by an act of departure. It is a departure that, in the full force of its historicity, remains at the same time in some sense absolutely opaque, both to the one who leaves and also to the theoretician, linked to the sufferer in his attempt to bring the experience to light. Yet at the same time, this very opacity generates the surprising force of a knowledge, for it is the accident, in German, *Unfall*, that reverberates in Freud's own theoretical insight drawn from the example, which is laced in the German with other forms of *fallen*, "to fall":

> As an afterthought it must strike us [*es muss uns auffallen*] that— in spite of the fundamental difference in the two cases [*Fälle*], the problem of the traumatic neurosis and that of Jewish monotheism—there is a correspondence in one point. It is the feature which one might term *latency*. There are the best grounds for thinking that in the history of the Jewish religion there is a long period, after the breaking away [*Abfall*] from the Moses religion, during which no trace is to be found of the monotheistic idea.[14]

Between the *Unfall*, the accident, and the "striking" of the insight, its *auffallen*, is the force of a fall, a falling that is transmitted precisely in the unconscious act of leaving. It is this unconsciousness of leaving that bears the impact of history. And it is likewise first of all in the unconsciousness of Freud's reference to his departure in his own text that, I would suggest, we first have access to its historical truth.

The full impact of this history occurs for us, however, in yet another aspect of the act of leaving, in what Freud calls "freedom." In the "Summary and Recapitulation" Freud says:

> It forced me to leave my home, but it also freed me of the fear lest my publishing the book might cause psychoanalysis to be forbidden in a country where its practice was still allowed.

Leaving home, for Freud, is also a kind of freedom, the freedom to bring forth his book in England, the freedom, that is, to bring his voice to another place. The meaning of this act is suggested in a letter that resonates with these lines from the "Summary," a letter written by Freud to his son Ernst in May 1938, while Freud was waiting for final arrangements to leave Vienna:

> Two prospects keep me going in these grim times: to rejoin you all and—to die in freedom.[15]

Freud's freedom to leave is, paradoxically, the freedom not to live but to die: to bring forth his voice to others in dying. Freud's voice emerges, that is, as a departure.[16] And it is this departure that, moreover, addresses us.

In the line he writes to his son, the last four words—"to die in freedom"—unlike the rest of the sentence, are not written in German, but rather in English. The announcement of his freedom, and of his dying, is given in a language that can be heard by those in the new place to which he brings his voice, to us, upon whom the legacy of psychoanalysis is bestowed. It is significant, moreover, that this message is conveyed not merely in the new language, English, but precisely in the movement between German and English, between the languages of the readers of his homeland and of his departure. I would like to suggest that it is here, in the movement from German to English, in the rewriting of the departure within the languages of Freud's text, that we participate most fully in Freud's central insight, in *Moses and Monotheism*, that history, like trauma, is never simply one's own, that history is precisely the way we are implicated in each other's traumas. For we—whether as German- or as English-speaking readers—cannot read this sentence without, ourselves, departing. In this departure, in the leave-taking of our hearing, we are first fully addressed by Freud's text, in ways we perhaps cannot yet fully understand. And, I would propose today, as we consider the possibilities of cultural and political analysis, that the impact of this not fully conscious address may be not only a valid but indeed a necessary point of departure.[17]

2 LITERATURE AND THE ENACTMENT OF MEMORY

(Duras, Resnais, *Hiroshima mon amour*)

And now each knows that in the act of survival he lived a dozen lives and saw more death than he ever thought he would see. At the same time, none of them knew anything.

John Hersey, *Hiroshima*

The surprising opening sequence of the 1959 French film *Hiroshima mon amour* (by Alain Resnais and Marguerite Duras) begins, after title and credits, with two alternating shots we do not fully comprehend: in the first shot, two interlaced elbows, arms, and a hand, their sagging skin covered with ash, then sweat, move in a slow embrace—apparently victims of the first atomic bombing of Hiroshima. This is followed by two intact elbows, arms, and a hand, first smooth, then sweaty, locked in an act of love—an intimate encounter taking place, as we will soon discover, between a French woman and a Japanese man, who have met by chance in Hiroshima, and whose passionate encounter will form the core of the film's narrative. Confronting us with these two alternating shots, the film immediately imposes on our sight and understanding several fundamental questions: What do the dying bodies of the past—the dying bodies of Hiroshima—have to do with the living bodies of the present? And what is the role of our seeing in establishing a relation between these two sets of bodies? Introducing its filmic narrative through these problems, *Hiroshima mon amour* opens up the question of history, I would propose, as an exploration of the relation between history and the body.

The question of history in this film, however, is a matter not only of what we see and know but also of what it is ethical to tell. The action of the film is itself the story of a telling, the story of a French actress who has come to make a film in Hiroshima and who, in her chance and passionate encounter with a Japanese man, tells for the first time in her life the story of her past: of her love affair at Nevers with a German soldier during the Occupation, of his death on the very day they were to run away together, which turned out to be the day of liberation; of her subsequent punishment, by the French townspeople, who shave her head, and by her parents, who trap her in a cellar, and finally of her ensuing madness.

After telling her story for the first time to her Japanese lover, toward the end of the film, the woman bemoans the action she has taken in an address to her dead German lover:

> I told our story.
> I was unfaithful to you tonight with this stranger.
> I told our story.
> It was, you see, a story that could be told. (73)[1]

Telling the story of her love affair with the German, telling, specifically, the story of his death, is for the woman a betrayal of the loved one, a betrayal of the one who died, with the one who is alive and listens. What the woman mourns is not only an erotic betrayal, that is, but a betrayal precisely in the act of telling, in the very transmission of an understanding that erases the specificity of a death. The possibility of knowing history, in this film, is thus also raised as a deeply ethical dilemma: the unremitting problem of *how not to betray the past.*

It would appear to be this problem of betrayal that is also at the heart of the film's own innovative method, which, while naming Hiroshima in its title, does not tell the story of Hiroshima in 1945 but rather uses the rebuilt Hiroshima as the setting for the telling of another story, the French woman's story of Nevers. The filmmaker Alain Resnais had originally been commissioned to make a documentary on Hiroshima, but after several months of collecting archival footage he had refused to carry out the project, claiming that such a film would not significantly differ from his previous documentary on concentration camps *(Nuit et brouillard).*[2] In his refusal to make a documentary on Hiroshima, Resnais paradoxically implies that it is direct archival footage that cannot maintain the very specificity of the event. And it would appear, equally paradoxically, that it is through the fictional story, not *about* Hiroshima but taking place at its site, that Resnais and Duras believe such historical specificity is conveyed. I would suggest that the interest of *Hiroshima mon amour* lies in how it explores the possibility of a faithful history in the very indirectness of this telling.

■ THE BETRAYAL OF SIGHT

The encounter between the French woman and the Japanese man emerges, at the opening of the film, in a disagreement about the possibility of communicating history, a conflict that focuses precisely on the nature of seeing, and specifically on the seeing of the body. Over the opening shot of the lovemaking bodies we hear first, in French (the language of the film), the voice of a man followed by that of a woman:

> He: You saw nothing in Hiroshima. Nothing.
> She: I saw *everything. Everything.* (15)

Coming from a Japanese man at Hiroshima, the denial of the woman's seeing is also, implicitly, a powerful assertion of what the man, in effect, *has* seen. What he apparently has seen, moreover, appears, as the film continues, on the screen before us, in the shots of mutilated bodies at the museum, in archival footage, and in the hospital the woman says she has visited. But paradoxically enough, his denial of her seeing, set against this background, suggests that the difference between what she does not see and what he does see is not merely a matter of empirical perception:

> She: The hospital for instance, I saw it. I'm sure I did. How could I help seeing it?
> He: You did not see the hospital in Hiroshima. You saw nothing in Hiroshima.
> She: Four times at the museum. . . .
> He: What museum in Hiroshima? (15–17)

The man's negation, aimed not only at the woman but at the very shots of wounded bodies on the screen, suggests that the problem with the woman's sight is not what she does not perceive, but *that* she perceives, precisely, a *what:*

> She: I've always wept over the fate of Hiroshima. Always.
> He: No. What would you have cried about?
> [Non. Sur *quoi* aurais-tu pleuré?] (18; 26)

Set against the pictures of the wounded, and directed at the repeated recitations of "I saw," the man's denial suggests that the act of seeing, in the very establishing of a bodily referent, erases, like an empty grammar, the reality of an event.[3] Within the insistent grammar of sight, the man suggests, the body erases the event of its own death.

This effacement of the event of Hiroshima in the very sight and understanding of the woman also constitutes, within the opening dialogue, her understanding of Hiroshima from the perspective of a national French history:

> He: What did Hiroshima mean for you, in France?
> She: The end of the war, I mean, really the end. . . .
> He: The whole world was happy. You were happy with the whole world. (33–34)

For the French, Hiroshima did not signify the beginning of the suffering of the Japanese, but rather precisely the end of their own suffering. The knowledge of Hiroshima, for the French, understood not as the incomprehensible occurrence of the nuclear bombing of the Japanese but as the knowledge they call "the end," effaces the event of a Japanese past and inscribes it, as a referent, into the narrative of French history.[4] And this inscription of the Japanese event into the history of the French— the inevitable self-referential reversal of the act of understanding, founded in the erasure of death—is also associated, in the dialogue, with a kind of *moral* betrayal within the act of sight, with, indeed, the filming of Hiroshima, which the French woman, as an actress, has come to do:

> He: What's the film you're playing in?
> She: A film about Peace. What else do you expect them to make in Hiroshima except a picture about Peace? (34)

Just as the French understand the event of Hiroshima as the end of their own war, so the perception of Hiroshima itself, from the perspective of an international history, turns the very actuality of catastrophe into the anonymous narrative of peace.[5]

In its emphasis on this inevitable inscription of the event of a catastrophe in the generality of another's history, *Hiroshima mon amour* would thus seem to reveal the necessity of betrayal in the ineluctability of sight.

It is indeed the necessary betrayal of the particular past in the understanding of a history that constitutes the story the French woman comes to tell the man, and that serves to make the story of Nevers the one story that can be told at Hiroshima. At the center of her story, as she finally reveals it, is the irony of the fact that it is on the very day of France's liberation that her German lover, waiting to flee with her from France, is shot just before she comes to meet him. The focal point of her story is the simultaneous occurrence of the event of liberation and the event of his death:

> I stayed near his body all that day and then all the next night. The next morning they came to pick him up and they put him in a truck. It was that night Nevers was liberated. The bells of St. Etienne were ringing, ringing . . . Little by little he grew cold beneath me. (65)

The death of her lover is not only temporally simultaneous with the day of liberation, it is also a part of what theoretically has made liberation possible, the murder of the "enemy." This translation of a murder into the knowledge of liberation is represented in her story by the ringing of the bells—the knowledge of the time of liberation and the moment in a history that covers over, precisely, the dying of her lover's body, the event of his death.

Similarly, the woman's story of her forced entrance into the cellar as punishment by the French is essentially a representation of her own attempt, in her entrance into madness, to maintain the event of death against the understanding of liberation. This faithfulness to her lover's death takes place through the

mutilation of her body as she hears the "deafening" sound of
the *Marseillaise* being played above her underground cell:

> Hands become useless in cellars. They scrape. They rub the skin
> off . . . against the walls. . . . that's all you can find to do, to make
> you feel better . . . and also to remember. . . I loved blood since
> I had tasted yours. (55)

Not unlike the Japanese man's refusal of her sight at Hiroshima
("You saw nothing"), the woman's faithfulness to her dead German lover occurs through the refusal of sight and understanding, but a refusal that, unlike his, takes place literally in relation
to her own body. Her refusal is thus carried out in the body's
fragmentation, in the separation of her hands from the rest of
her corporeal self and in the communion with her lover's death
through the sucking of her own blood. It is thus utterly deprived
of sight and understanding, and only as a fragment, that the body
can become, for the woman, the faithful monument to a death.

It is likewise the unavoidable reintegration of the body in
the recovery of her hands that represents in this story a betrayal
in the forgetting imposed by the sight and understanding of a
larger history:

> My hair is growing back. I can feel it every day, with my hand. I
> don't care. But nevertheless my hair is growing back . . . .
>
> At six in the evening, the bells of St. Etienne Cathedral ring,
> winter and summer. One day, it is true, I hear them. I remember
> having heard them before—before—when we were in love, when
> we were happy.
>
> I'm beginning to see.
>
> I remember having already seen before—before—when we
> were in love, when we were happy.
>
> I remember.
>
> I see the ink.
>
> I see the daylight.
>
> I see my life. Your death.

> My life that goes on. Your death that goes on. . . .
> Oh! It's horrible. I'm beginning to remember you less clearly. I'm beginning to forget you. I tremble at the thought of having forgotten so much love . . . (61, 63–64)

In this story of a past, it is not just the false knowledge of others but the very movement of the woman's own consciousness that acts as the betrayal of love, as the forgetting of her own lover's death. Indeed, this forgetting is enacted in her use of *voir*, "to see," which begins as a literal perception, "I see the ink," and ends as a figure of knowing, "I see my life. Your death." Recalling her insistent seeing of Hiroshima, the insistence of her seeing in this story, as the inevitable movement from literal to figurative sight or understanding, subsumes the event of death in the continuous history of her life. Seeing thus inaugurates the forgetting of the singularity of her lover by forgetting the referential specificity of his death. Just as the entrance into the cellar represents the faithfulness of madness, the story of her exit from the cellar—which resonates, in the French word *cave*, with the Platonic story of the cave—comes to mean the emergence into a full, truer knowledge that forgetting is indeed a necessary part of understanding.[6]

This truth is also, for the woman, the complicity of understanding with the falseness of a certain kind of freedom:

> I think then is when I got over my hate. I don't scream any more. I'm becoming reasonable. They say: "She's becoming reasonable." One night, a holiday, they let me go out. (66)

To be reasonable here is no longer to cling madly to the memory of the lover's death; it is to exit into the freedom of forgetting.[7] This freedom, like her seeing, is also enacted in her own language, which transforms the literal exiting from the cellar into the figurative exiting from hate: "I think that is when I got over my hate" [Je crois que c'est à ce moment-là que je suis sortie de la méchanceté ("that I exited from my hate")]. Freedom from madness is thus equated with the forgetting that began her sane seeing and knowing, a freedom that is fundamentally a betrayal of the past.

The movement of this freedom is also characterized as an arrival, a symbolic arrival of the woman at a common site and a common moment of French history; she is let out "on a holiday," a day that commemorates, presumably, an event such as liberation. And notably, it is her insertion into a national time that also marks, for her, a relation to the history of others, and specifically, to the events at Hiroshima:

> When I reach Paris two days later the name of Hiroshima is in all the newspapers.
>
> [Quand j'arrive à Paris, le surlendemain, le nom Hiroshima est sur tous les journaux.] (67; 101–2)

Telling the "when" of her arrival in Paris as the moment that she learned of Hiroshima, the woman connects her own arrival, her insertion into collective French time, with a factual knowledge of Japan's catastrophe, which, as she has said before, has meant for her only "the end of the war." The arrival into national history thus erases not only her past but that of other nations as well. Ending with the decisive act of her reintegrated body—she arrives in Paris on a bicycle—the story implies that the erasure of the event takes place in the historical and social situation of the integrated body.[8] And it is through precisely this erasure of her past that she can see and "know" the past of others as well, the past of Hiroshima as much as the past of Nevers. In telling her story of Nevers, the woman thus seems to reinterpret her earlier claims to see and to know Hiroshima as essentially at one with the man's denials: Hiroshima and Nevers are linked, in their very forgetting, through the ceaseless betrayal of bodily sight.

■ "LISTEN TO ME"

Yet if the film seems to isolate memory within the all of madness and the nothing of forgetting, it also invokes these extremes at the very opening of a dialogue, and asks what might become possible within a discourse that is not simply *about* Hiroshima (or Nevers), but within an encounter that takes place *at* Hiroshima, a discourse spoken, as it were, *on the site of a catastrophe.* Within the context of her own story, the woman's "I saw everything" is not simply the claim to know all about Hiroshima, but a claim to have faithfully remembered Nevers. Between the man's "nothing" and the woman's "everything" is not, then, simply an opposition about what she does or does not see of Hiroshima, but the coming together of two absolute claims to faithfulness—to Hiroshima and to Nevers. The problem of knowing Hiroshima is not simply the problem of an outsider's knowing the inside of another's experience; more profoundly, the film dramatizes something that happens when two different experiences, absolutely alien to one another, are brought together:

> She: . . . Listen to me.
>   Like you, I know what it is to forget. . . .
>   Like you, I have a memory. I know what it is to forget. . . .
>   Like you, I too have tried with all my might not to forget. Like you, I forgot. Like you, I wanted to have an inconsolable memory, a memory of shadows and stone.
>   For my part, I struggled with all my might, every day, against the horror of no longer understanding at all the reason for remembering. Like you, I forgot.
>   Why deny the obvious necessity for memory? (22–23)

The similarity between Hiroshima and Nevers is not only an analogy, "like you," but an address: "listen to me." Within this address, the forgetting of Hiroshima and Nevers is also a claim to a discovered and not fully comprehensible knowledge, "I know what it is to forget" [Je connais l'oubli]. The knowledge

of forgetting here is not something owned, that is, but something *addressed to another*, addressed not simply as a fact, but as
a command—"Listen to me"—and as a question—"Why deny
the obvious necessity for memory?" The words "like you," that
is, spoken in the context of disaster, do not necessarily only state
the banal truth of an already given likeness, but demand a listening, and ask for memory as a question. Not simply spoken
after Hiroshima, but spoken *on the site of* Hiroshima, the words
of the encounter establish an opening, not only through their
meaning, but in the performance of a command that breaks their
meaning and in the question that this disruption opens.

The encounter at Hiroshima, as it unfolds in the film, thus
emerges not as an exchange of histories, but as the disruption of
the sight and knowledge of the woman in her very telling of the
story of Nevers:

> No, you don't know what it is to forget. . . . No, you don't have
> a memory. (23)

The man's challenge to the woman's memory is not a simple
denial of what she does or can remember but, paradoxically, a
denial of both her memory and her forgetting: a denial, that is,
that she can simply know, and tell, the difference between remembering and what it is to forget. From this perspective, likewise, his insistence that she "saw nothing" at Hiroshima does
not so much reassert the clarity of his sight as it addresses what,
in her, is *not simple* about seeing. Indeed, the scene in which her
story first unfolds begins with her encounter with a mode of
seeing that is neither precisely remembering nor forgetting:

> She: What were you dreaming about?
> He: I don't remember. . . . Why?
> She: I was looking at your hands. They move when you're
>   asleep.
> He: Maybe it's when you dream without knowing it. (29)

The man's forgetting of the dream here does not so much concern the fact that one might not know *what* one has dreamed as it opens up the possibility that one might not know *that* one is dreaming; that one might see, that is, without knowing it. This seeing, moreover, unlike the seeing whose appearance and disappearance mark the passage of time in the woman's story, itself constitutes a time *of* not knowing: "Maybe it's when you dream without knowing it" [C'est quand on rêve, peut-être, sans le savoir].

In fact, just such a seeing has arisen cinematically in how the woman looks at the sleeping Japanese man, and specifically, in how she sees his body and, more precisely, his hands: "I was looking at your hands." In a series of shots that precede this exchange, the film first introduces into its visual sequence an uncertainty of seeing linked to the woman's gaze upon the man: after passing from the image of her intent face to the barely moving hand of the sleeping man at whom she stares, the shot switches suddenly, for just a flash, to the twitching hand of another man, upon the ground, then to a young woman kissing the bloody, supine face, then back to the sleeping man upon the bed. In the juxtaposition of hands—a series of images that is presumably seen by the woman, and that the spectator sees without quite grasping them and without understanding—we are first introduced, in sight, to the event that forms her story, to the death of her German lover (whom the woman apparently sees while looking at the hand of the Japanese man).[9] But if the woman is opened to a past here through what she sees, it is not in how the living body at Hiroshima represents for her the knowledge of the dead—how the sight of the living body represents and replaces the body of the dead—but in the uncanny similarity that the seen body, the hand, reveals between the unconsciousness of sleeping and the unconsciousness of dying.[10] Seeing, here, as a seeing of the body, is what cannot tell the difference between living and dying. Rather than erasing, in the movement from literal to figurative seeing, the reality of a death, the woman's literal seeing precisely introduces, in its radical confusion, the death of her German lover into the sight of the living body of the man she sees. As it occurs in the process of the encounter, the woman's seeing is not the erasure of a death that was once known, but the continual reappearance of a death she has not quite grasped, the reemergence, in sight, of her *not knowing* the difference between life and death.

A QUESTION OF LIFE AND DEATH

It is indeed the question of this difference that, framing her closed narrative of remembering and forgetting, opens up the woman's history. It opens it up, however, not by asking for a knowledge she owns and can thus simply state within her story, but by calling upon the movement of her not knowing within the very language of her telling. When the man begins the questioning that leads to her final telling of her story, he does not ask about the lover's death as a fact she could know; rather, by assuming the position of the lover himself, he asks her to speak of his death through the very impossibility of distinguishing the living from the dead:

When you are in the cellar, am I dead?

[Quand tu es dans la cave, je suis mort?] (54; 87)

Asked as if it were possible to answer, this question first reduces the whole story of the woman's past, the whole truth of her history, to the telling of a single time, the "when" [quand] of her lover's death. The "when," as *the* question of history, is the difference between life and death. Yet, spoken within the living man's assumption of the dead man's voice, the question recognizes that the answer cannot simply be spoken, that the possibility of this knowledge can only arise within the very act of its denial; that the woman cannot know the death of her loved one, that is, without sharing this knowledge, and addressing this story, to him. Her not knowing, as the man's question calls upon it, is an endless address to her dead lover. And it is only from the perspective of this death, assumed by the man who listens, that her story can be heard.

What she comes to tell is likewise both the story of her confrontation with her lover's death and an appeal to the impossibility of such a confrontation:

> We were supposed to meet at noon on the quay of the Loire. I was going to leave with him. When I arrived at noon on the quay of the Loire, he wasn't quite dead yet. Someone had fired on him from a garden.
>
> I stayed near his body all that day and then all the next night. The next morning they came to pick him up and they put him in a truck. It was that night Nevers was liberated. The bells of St. Etienne were ringing, ringing . . . Little by little he grew cold beneath me. Oh! how long it took him to die! When? I'm not quite sure. I was lying on top of him . . . yes . . . the moment of his death actually escaped me, because . . . because even at that very moment, and even afterward, yes, even afterward, I can say that I couldn't feel the slightest difference between this dead body and mine. All I could find between this body and mine were obvious similarities, do you understand? (Shouting) He was my first love . . . . (64–65)

Speaking of her first sight of the dying soldier, what she in fact tells of is not the sight of death itself but rather, and more terribly, the shock of her encounter with the passage from life to death: "When I arrived at noon on the quay of the Loire, he wasn't quite dead yet" [Quand je suis arrivée à midi sur le quai de la Loire il n'était pas tout à fait mort]. Indeed, while it is framed as a simple narrative beginning ("when I arrived at noon"), the very immediacy of this sight, the "when" of its occurrence, becomes at once, in her telling, the very inability to know the moment of his death: "When? I'm not quite sure. . . . the moment of his death actually escaped me" [Quand? Je ne sais plus au juste. . . . le moment de sa mort m'a échappé vraiment]. Between the "when" of seeing his dying and the "when" of his actual death there is an unbridgeable abyss, an inherent gap of knowing, within the very immediacy of sight, the moment of the other's death.

This missing of the "when" within the shock of sight is also experienced as a confusion of the body; for in missing the moment of his death, the woman is also unable to recognize the continuation of her life: "I couldn't feel the slightest difference between this dead body and mine. All I could find between this body and mine were obvious similarities, do you understand?" As the culmination of her story, the body marks the very transformation, in her own telling, from the shock of an arrival at an utterly singular and irrefutable moment—"Quand je suis arrivée à midi sur le quai"—into an endless impossibility of arriving—"Je n'arrivais pas à trouver la moindre différence entre ce corps mort et le mien." Her bodily life, that is, has become the endless attempt to witness her lover's death.[11] Her final address—"do you understand?"—spoken from within this eternity, no longer truly knows a history of loss, but rather speaks, beyond its knowing, the impossibility, precisely, of having her own history.

THE BEGINNING OF A HISTORY

The truth of the woman's story thus emerges not only in the power of its reference, but in the address that enacts the impossibility of her history. Yet it is also precisely within what this address cannot fully know that the possibility of another history opens up. For the solicitation "do you understand," in distinguishing the "you" momentarily from the dead body, responds to another, implicit dimension within the very words of the Japanese man's question, "Am I dead?" Within the very confusion that the question, by both addressing the French woman and apostrophizing the girl of Nevers, creates between the German soldier and the Japanese man, the words "am I dead?" curiously enough introduce into the dialogue the reality of the Japanese man himself, who does not simply assume figuratively the "I" of the dead German soldier but also refers to himself as what is still a question, as what has not been determined in his own life. For, as we discover in an earlier exchange in the film, the man who insists that the woman has seen nothing at Hiroshima does not do so precisely from the position of his own seeing:

> She: You were here, at Hiroshima. . . .
> He: No. . . Of course I wasn't.
> She: That's true. . . . How stupid of me.
> He: But my family was at Hiroshima. I was off fighting the war.
>   (28)

The Japanese man has, himself, missed the catastrophe at Hiroshima. What he knows, therefore, of his story, as he enters the dialogue with the French woman, is that he himself "saw nothing" at Hiroshima. Yet this missing of the event, a missing that is different from the woman's, resonates with hers in the passion of its argument and in his reference to his family. Through its very missing, his story, like hers, bears the impact of a trauma.

The man can step into the woman's story, then, when he poses his question of life and death only because he can, and perhaps in some way must, ask of her the question of his own survival: "When you are in the cellar, am I dead?" He listens to her, that is, out of his own not knowing, out of the impossibility of confrontation with his own past, and out of the lack of self that is spoken in his question. And it is precisely because he speaks from this impossible place, and asks a question that he himself does not fully own, that he can also enter her story, that he makes the answer to her story speak more than it can possibly tell. Not because he knows her truth but because he *does not know* his own, he can discover, even as she tells him of the impossibility of her own life, the survival of another for whom she unwittingly speaks in the double testimony of her response.

THE SIGNIFICANCE OF THE EXCHANGE

Because the lovers are thus linked in the missing of their traumas, what takes place in their dialogue is the establishment of their respective histories. This establishment of history, however, is not simply an act of empathy or understanding. From the beginning, the man has refused the woman's tears over the fate of Hiroshima in much the same way as the woman herself had, earlier in her life, refused her mother:

> She: I've always wept over the fate of Hiroshima. Always.
> He: No. What would you have cried about? (18)[12]

The tears of empathy here are refused by the man as a kind of misunderstanding. But in this dialogue, as we have seen, the refusal is not simply the isolation of two opposed and locked understandings. It rather constitutes the very heart of their link to each other. It is indeed at the climax of the narration of her story that her request for understanding and its refusal by him mark precisely the possibility of their connection:

> . . . All I could find between this body and mine were obvious similarities, do you understand? *(Shouting.)* He was my first love
> . . . . *(The Japanese slaps her. . . . She acts as though she didn't know where it had come from. But she snaps out of it, and acts as though she realized it had been necessary.)* (65–66)

As a response to her request for understanding, for understanding the impossibility of distinguishing the dead body from her own, the man's slap is a refusal of understanding, a refusal of empathy that, on the level of immediate experience and emotions, is experienced as an act of violence. But on the level of the address, and within the significance of the dialogue, the slap constitutes the imperative of distinguishing between life and death. This imperative is not truly experienced as a *knowing* of that crucial difference but as a *break* within the apostrophe, a disruption of the apostrophic—or prosopopoeic—confusion, in the woman's sight of the living body and in her address to the Japanese man as the dead soldier, which robbed both the Japanese man and the French woman of a history, and which joined them only in their absence within their own stories.[13]

What takes place in the disruption of the slap, then, is precisely the beginning of a history. It takes place, moreover, in a body that is seen, in the hand, precisely, that, raised to her face, no longer permits the confusion between her life and the German soldier's death, because it does not permit the confusion of his death with the Japanese man's life. This marking of a difference does not take place, indeed, in a corrected seeing or in the mere physical reality of a seen hand, but in the very way in which the hand, in its slap, surprises sight and interrupts the continuity of the face-to-face encounter of the lovers locked in a narrative-without-history. The slap indeed interrupts the pathos and the ahistorical sense of "firstness" in the cry—"He was my first love"—and thus interrupts the isolated self-enclosure of the narrative of firsts: a narrative that, incidentally, would include Hiroshima as the place in which the first atomic bomb was dropped.

This interruption and this *shock of sight* thus establishes within the film the opening of a history that had not yet truly taken place. The possibility of history arises, indeed, within this movement of the film, as the interruption of understanding in a brutal shock of sight that ineluctably connects the history of Nevers with that of Hiroshima. The traumatic histories of the two lovers can emerge, that is, only in their relation to each other and only in the way in which this relation creates, precisely, a break within the mutual understanding of their address.[14]

▊ THE OTHER'S STORY

The film does not end, however, with the completion of the woman's story. The last, somewhat enigmatic, scenes of the film focus, rather, on the woman's silent attempt to separate from her new lover as she prepares to depart from Hiroshima. In their first encounter after the climactic scene of the confession and the slap in the café, they meet in a train station, where the woman has wandered by herself, and where she has been followed by the man, who does not invade her privacy but sits down on the bench not far from her, separated from her by an old Japanese woman. Rather than conversing with his lover, the Japanese man watches her in silence until he is interrupted by the Japanese woman. Their conversation, in Japanese, remains untranslated— and with no subtitles—in the film. In the written, published script, the conversation is transcribed as follows:

Vieille Femme: Qui c'est?
[The Old Woman: Who is she?]

Lui: Une Française.
[He: A French woman.]

Vieille Femme: Qu'est-ce qu'il y a?
[The Old Woman: What's the matter?]

Lui: Elle va quitter le Japan tout à l'heure. Nous sommes tristes de nous quitter.
[He: She's leaving Japan in a little while. We're sad at having to leave each other.] (120, 80)

As it is represented in this scene, the separation of the man and the woman in the film is not simply an ending, but leads also, implicitly, to the introduction of a new story and a new language: the story told by the Japanese man, spoken in a language native to him but new to the film and foreign to the French woman as well as to most of the audience at whom the film is aimed. The story of the man, as he tells it to his own compatriot, is the story told by the film itself, the story of his relationship with, or more specifically, his separation from, the woman. But as this story of the ending comes to us in translation, its language, Japanese, does not represent a simple break from the language and the story of the woman. It also constitutes, in resonance with her own narrative, another language of departure: a language of *quitter* and of *leaving*—"Elle va quitter le Japon tout à l'heure; nous sommes tristes de nous quitter" [She's leaving Japan in a little while. We're sad at having to leave each other]. The closing of the woman's story of departure is also, then, the opening of a question about the man: about the possibility, for those who listen, of precisely understanding what it means to depart; of understanding, that is, the language of the Japanese man's own trauma.[15]

THE SPECTATOR AND THE QUESTION OF LANGUAGE

The element of incomprehensibility introduced by the sound of the Japanese does not, however, merely signal the inaccessibility of another culture, but draws in the spectator of the film as a participant in its action and as a part of the complex attempt to know—or to come to know—Hiroshima. The old Japanese woman to whom the man speaks is herself, above all, a spectator of the relationship between the two lovers, and her question, "Who is she?" is the film's first explicit representation of what it means to watch this film and to question it, a watching and a questioning that, notably, takes places in a language that does not fully belong to the action of the film. An analogous representation had already, implicitly, arisen with the occurrence of the slap in the scene at the café, at the climax of the telling of the woman's story. For at this moment of the slap, the camera pans quickly to the faces of the Japanese customers at the bar, all of whom suddenly turn toward the couple in surprise at the unexpectedly loud and explosive sound. The sound of the slap thus breaks the private bond of the two lovers and introduces into their passionate intimacy the eyes and ears of others.

Paradoxically, these strangers are linked to the lovers precisely through what they do not comprehend. Indeed the surprise of the sound of the slap first draws into the scene, and incorporates within the film as a whole, the relationship between the Japanese man and his own compatriots, who, from their own perspective, hear him speak a language not his own. Simultaneously, the scene introduces the spectators of the film as those who not only watch but listen, and whose understanding of Hiroshima must pass through the fiction of the film and through the multiplicity of the languages it speaks. Indeed, the scenes that follow the slap can be said to reintroduce the questions raised by the opening of the film, the problem of knowing Hiroshima not only as what can be seen and understood in the body but also as what can be heard and understood in the voice that speaks through it.

The spectators' language is, however, not only Japanese. After the scene at the train station, the man follows the French actress through the streets of Hiroshima into a cocktail lounge, a café called Casablanca. Seating himself apart from her, he watches and listens as she is approached by another Japanese man, a stranger who assumes she is a tourist and tries to pick her up by speaking to her in English, with the following words, which again remain untranslated in the film (and appear as follows in both the French and English texts):

> Are you alone?
> It is very late to be lonely.
> May I sit down? Are you just visiting Hiroshima?
> Do you like Japan?
> Do you live in Paris? (81)[16]

The sound of the English, following closely upon the Japanese spoken by the man and the old woman at the train station, acts as yet another sign of the separation and imminent departure of the woman, through the intrusion of a language that belongs to neither of the two lovers. The English, like the Japanese, seems to represent their separation through the intrusion of others and through the link between the Japanese man and a Japanese perspective that divides him from her. Yet the English, spoken in short, memorized guidebook phrases by a Japanese man who clearly does not know the language well, and observed in turn by a Japanese man who may or may not know this language, also suggests that the Japanese perspective (and, indeed, the perspective of the film) may not have a single accessible language of its own. If this scene, like the ones before it, opens up the possibility of the Japanese man's history beyond the French woman's departure, it does so only within an address to those who speak another language, and who view the story—and the film—from the perspective of another past.

CAFÉ CASABLANCA, OR THE CINEMATIC PAST

This language and this past themselves are not anonymous. In a film appearing, as did *Hiroshima mon amour*, in 1959, the café Casablanca, in which this scene takes place, cannot but be understood as an allusion to the American classic of 1942, *Casablanca*, a World War II film that centers on a café in Casablanca, a café called Rick's Café Americain. The Casablanca in *Hiroshima mon amour* can thus be considered, through its allusion to the French name of the café in the American film, a version of the Café Americain. And the English spoken here is, likewise, an address to those whose history, like that of the Japanese, is also tied to the catastrophic event at Hiroshima, an address to the Americans, who so far have been virtually absent from the film. The history of the Japanese man is not directly told, that is, but is elliptically suggested as an address to the listening and to the hearing of the Americans who watch the film. His story can be told, that is, only when the Americans can hear, through the speaking of their own language by the Japanese and through the translation of their own fiction into the fiction of others, the story of their own reality, not yet recognized but introduced, as a question, into the fiction of the address.

The Americans are thus addressed not directly as participants in the events of the past but rather as spectators, as viewers of a fictional film. They are addressed, that is, in this fiction, through their indirect relation to their own history.

In *Casablanca* this fiction was indeed, specifically, the story of a departure. Set in Casablanca, which is described as the last point of passage from "imprisoned Europe" to the free world, and taking place specifically in Rick's Café Americain, where exit visas are illegally sold, the film follows the story of an American named Rick, who, unable to return to the United States himself, makes possible the departures of others and, ultimately, of the very woman he loves and of her husband, a resistance fighter fleeing the Nazis and the French Vichy collaborators who have cornered him at Casablanca.

The film *Casablanca* thus represents the Americans as the liberators of Europe. But this fiction was itself less a depiction of a truth already in existence than an attempt to address an America that was not yet, in fact, playing the role of liberator: when the film was made in 1942, Roosevelt, against Churchill's advice, was still reluctant to withdraw support from the Vichy government in France. It has been suggested that *Casablanca* was in fact used as propaganda aimed at enlisting his support for de Gaulle, in which task it was successful (the film was shown at the White House on New Year's Eve, 1942–1943).[17] If, in its political drama of departure, the film represents the successful liberation of Europeans by the Americans, it nonetheless offers its representation in the service of an address to what it conceives as America's own blindness. This blindness was even apparent, as it has been noted, in two of its most famous lines, the only lines that name the time of the action of the film itself: in his dialogue with the black piano player Louis, Rick says, "If it's December 1941 in Casablanca, what time is it in New York? . . . I bet they're asleep in New York, I bet they're asleep all over America."[18] In his own fictional, representational role as the American who liberates Europe, the character Rick also addresses those of his compatriots who have not awoken from their sleep, or from their blindness to the urgency of shifting foreign policy in the war. Even in its retrospective representation, *Casablanca* serves not only as a depiction of America's liberating action but as a continual reminder, an address concerning the necessity of awakening to what Americans have not yet seen of their participation in the war.

In its transposition to the café in Hiroshima, the story of *Casablanca* thus resonates with what the American film touches on but cannot know in the history of the war: the other side of "December 1941," the final stage of the war that develops between the Japanese and the Americans and concludes with the dropping of the bombs on Hiroshima and Nagasaki in August 1945. Casablanca, as the name of a Japanese café, essentially calls forth the other side of what seemed, in the American film, a simple passage to freedom: "Now I know," says the resistance fighter to Rick as he leaves Casablanca, "that our side will win."[19] Located in post-Hiroshima Japan, in a film made jointly by the French and the Japanese, the American representation of liberation from the enemy is returned in the form of its own blindness, the literal realization of the logic of liberation by which the understanding of one's own national identity has taken place through the forgetting, and obliteration, of the other.[20]

In the scene in which the Japanese protagonist watches the Japanese stranger approach his French lover with stereotypical expressions of a memorized English, the consequences of this forgetting can be said to take place in a double form. The intrusion of English implies, first of all, a gap within the bond of the Japanese in their common desire for a woman from the West:

this desire places the men at odds, since the woman's possible involvement with the new Japanese stranger signals her departure from her lover. But there is also, perhaps, a certain loss of self implicit in the speaking of another's language. In this respect, in spite of the difference in their linguistic skills, the Japanese lover can recognize in the stranger's use of English a symbol of his own speaking in French. English, in this scene, is the language of forgetting.

But the forgetting and the loss implied by the intrusion of English is equally a loss for the Americans, who can see and hear themselves only through the face and voice of the Japanese man, and, through the name of the café, in an allusion to their own culture translated into the terms of Japanese culture. If Americans can recognize themselves in *Hiroshima mon amour*, it would appear to be only in the fiction of a false resemblance— in the artificiality of a cultural takeover—that serves, precisely, as the forgetting of the event of Hiroshima. The relation between the Americans and the Japanese—a relation defined after 1945 first and foremost by the dropping of two atomic bombs— can only be perceived, it would seem, through a language of fiction, a fiction that inherently erases the reality of the past it conveys.[21]

EPILOGUE: THE PRODUCTION OF THE FILM, OR THE UNTRANSLATABILITY OF THE VOICE

I would suggest, however, that the final significance of *Hiroshima mon amour*, in its meditation on communication across traumatic and cultural boundaries, is not closed off with this self-reflective, critical dimension of the film. It is indeed interesting to note that the question of translation and of untranslatability played a role, as well, in the production of the film, and in the actual communication between the actors. In a 1986 interview about the film, Emmanuelle Riva—the actress who played the French actress in the film—described how the production of the film crossed the line between acting and living, or between fiction and reality, and how the very process of the making of the film was itself, for its participants, at once a rare achievement of cross-cultural communication and a unique experience of accoustic and linguistic difference:

> ER: As far as the work was concerned, we communicated totally. It became better and better because each day we entered fully into the story. Finally one's engagement with the work reached a point that the story of the film became one's own. I no longer made any distinction between the life of the film and real life. Oh no! It was my life. It meant everything. During the two months of shooting, I gave myself to it totally. Within some limits of course. And that was true of everyone. We spoke with each other incessantly in utter felicity. With the Japanese actor, the marvelous Eiji Okada, too, thanks to an interpreter. Same thing for the Japanese technicians. We were together, do you understand? Together. That was what was beautiful.
>
> I: You say that you communicated with your Japanese partner thanks to an interpreter. Then he didn't speak French?
>
> ER: Not a word. He learned everything phonetically. What a performance! But the most terrible thing was that we found out too late that our camera had made noise and that it was necessary to repeat the entire film. From A to Z. Can you imagine? Alain searched for a Japanese man in Paris who could lend his voice, but no one satisfied him. He had to make Eiji Okada come [from Japan] in order to begin again his linguistic exploit, and we repeated the entire film in the studio, taking the time that was necessary. But as you have seen, the work was remarkable.[22]

The Japanese man who speaks such beautiful French throughout the film (a fact that, at two points, is explicitly referred to in the script)[23] is played by a man who, in reality, knows no French whatsoever, a man who has not even truly memorized the textual lines that he recites, but who has memorized only their sounds, which, grammatically, make no sense to him at all. This fact is quite remarkable. Okada introduces a difference that he does not truly *act* through his role: The Japanese man speaking French in the story does not, that is, truly represent, in any mimetic or specular relation, the actor who plays him. Unlike the Japanese lover, who has learned a foreign language that momentarily takes over his own, the Japanese actor only voices the sounds of a language he has phonetically memorized. Far from absenting him, this voicing of sounds in fact distinguishes him from the fictional character whose well-learnt French represents, in part, the loss of the Japanese referent: Okada's memorization cannot be considered in the same terms of loss and forgetting. Okada, in other words, does not represent, but rather voices his difference quite literally, and untranslatably. What he contributes to the role is the unique concreteness of his voice. Okada thus introduces a mode of speaking that, quite in line with the philosophy and the profound human truth articulated by the film, does not *own* or master its own meaning, but uniquely transmits the difference of its voice.[24]

Indeed, as Emmanuelle Riva points out, it would appear to be precisely Eiji Okada's capacity to memorize purely phonetically that cannot be duplicated and that, when the film has to be remade, makes it necessary that Eiji Okada and no other be located and brought back from Japan, to repeat the whole unique experience of the making of the film, and to allow once more for the singularity—for the creative *difference*—of its effect. And it is the memory, precisely, of this singularity of voice and of effect that, in the interview itself, years later, still has the effect of creating the peculiar moment of a crossing between the fiction of the film and the mirror-action of the reminiscence that takes place in the reality of the interview itself: for it is precisely in her introduction of the need for an interpreter for Eiji Okada that Emmanuelle Riva turns to the interviewer with the very literal pathos of the words with which, as the French actress in the film, she turned to her lover: "With the Japanese actor, the marvelous Eiji Okada . . . thanks to an interpreter. . . . We were together, *do you understand?*"

In the film, she had said: "I can say that I couldn't feel the slightest difference between this dead body and mine. All I could find between this body and mine were obvious similarities, *do you understand?*" Against our understanding, the film interrupted, at that moment, the narrator's pathos in her plea for understanding, and the intimacy of her confession, by the explosive sound of the slap by which the Japanese man dramatized, in yet another concrete figure, the radical disjoining of sound from meaning through which the film's dialogue precisely speaks. And likewise Emmanuelle Riva's surprising revelation of Okada's phonetic feat helps us recognize that the sound of Okada's speaking, in its own disjunctive voicing or empty articulation, may introduce a specificity and singularity into the film that exceeds what it is able to convey on the level of its representation. And it is for this reason, indeed, that the final scenes of the film do not simply represent a loss of culture and history in the forgetting imposed by the assumption of a foreign language. For the voice of the Japanese actor bears witness to his resistant, irreducible singularity, and opens as a future possibility the telling of another history.[25]

ANOTHER HIROSHIMA

It is this actor's voice that, finally, returns to us from the opening scenes of the film, to interrupt once more our sight and understanding of the bodies that we see with a bodily voice that, once again, denies our facile empathy and our rush to comprehension, and demands a different kind of listening and a different speaking. In this speaking—a speaking literally of the body—we might hear, for example, another implicit emergence

of the Japanese story, in the form of a specific address, woven
within the opening argument of man and woman:

He: You saw nothing in Hiroshima. Nothing.
She: The reconstructions have been made as authentically as
   possible.
   The illusion, it's quite simple, the illusion is so perfect
   that the tourists cry.
   One can always scoff, but what else can a tourist do, really,
   but cry?
   I've always wept over the fate of Hiroshima. Always.
He: No. What would you have cried about?
She: I saw the newsreels.
   On the second day, History tells, I'm not making it up, on
   the second day certain species of animals rose again from the
   depths of the earth and from the ashes.
   Dogs were photographed.
   For all eternity.
   I saw them.
   I *saw* the newsreels.
   I *saw* them.
   On the first day.
   On the second day.
   On the third day.
He: You saw nothing. Nothing.
She: . . . on the fifteenth day too.
   Hiroshima was blanketed with flowers. There were corn-
   flowers and gladiolas everywhere, and morning glories and
   day lilies that rose again from the ashes with an extraordi-
   nary vigor, quite unheard of for flowers till then.*
   I didn't make anything up.
He: You made it *all* up.
She: *Nothing.*
   Just as in love this illusion exists, this illusion of being able
   never to forget, so I was under the illusion that I would
   never forget Hiroshima.
   Just as in love.

*This sentence is taken almost verbatim from John Hersey's admirable report on Hiroshima. All I did was apply it to the martyred children. (18–19)

Arguing for the intensity and the extremity of what she *has* seen, and implicitly for her communion in that horror and that misery through the unthinkable experience of her own madness in Nevers, the French-speaking woman cites, in translation, a striking sentence—an unsettling line from what was the first English-language text to introduce the human reality of Hiroshima to the American public: John Hersey's *Hiroshima*, published in the United States one year after the dropping of the atomic bombs. This original English-language text that *Hiroshima mon amour* recites in French was itself, moreover, to a certain extent a textual translation, an English transcription and rewriting of Japanese eyewitness reports. The echo of Hersey thus introduces into the film not only another possible address to Americans but a different Japanese perspective and a new mode of seeing.[26]

The line in Hersey's book about the wildflowers blooming in the devastated Hiroshima is indeed taken from a striking passage that, in the original text, is largely about seeing. It is narrated as part of the testimonial story of Miss Sasaki, who had to be moved from some other hospital to the Red Cross Hospital in Hiroshima because "her leg did not improve but swelled more and more." Hersey writes:

> This was the first chance she had had to look at the ruins of Hiroshima; the last time she had been carried through the city's streets, she had been hovering on the edge of unconsciousness. Even though the wreckage had been described to her, and though she was still in pain, the sight horrified and amazed her, and there was something she noticed about it that particularly gave her the creeps. Over everything—up through the wreckage of the city, in gutters, along the riverbanks, tangled among tiles and tin roofing, climbing on charred tree trunks—was a blanket of fresh,

vivid, lush, optimistic green; the verdancy rose even from the foundations of ruined houses. Weeds already hid the ashes, and wild flowers were in bloom among the city's bones. The bomb had not only left the underground organs of plants intact; it had stimulated them. Everywhere were bluets and Spanish bayonets, goosefoot, morning glories and day lilies, the hairy-fruited bean, purslane and clotbur and sesame and panic grass and feverfew. Especially in a circle at the center, sickle senna grew in extraordinary regeneration, not only standing among the charred remnants of the same plant but pushing up in new places, among bricks and through cracks in the asphalt. It actually seemed as if a load of sickle-senna seed had been dropped along with the bomb.[27]

Miss Sasaki's return to Hiroshima is a return to a new kind of vision. The whole text of Duras could be viewed, indeed, as a French translation, or rather, as a variation, on the story of this wounded woman: the story of a repetition of her "seeing Hiroshima," the first time from "the edge of unconsciousness," the second time regaining consciousness (even as the ravage of the wound persists) and "looking at the ruins" out of which the flowers sprout. Returning to the site of the catastrophe—which is also the site of unconsciousness (or, "the edge of unconsciousness")—Miss Sasaki now sees something that "gives her the creeps," the flowers "optimistically" growing over the ruins, a form of ongoing life inextricably bound up with the very act of destruction.

In the film, however, Marguerite Duras disturbs the second seeing by superimposing it on the first, by "transferring," as she puts it, the line about the sprouting flowers, onto the footage of the "burnt children screaming." In juxtaposing the "optimism" of the flowers growing over the ruins with the documents and reconstructions of the moments of the catastrophe, Duras emphasizes the catastrophic sight that remains disjoined and insistently returning along with the strange survival of life. And likewise, in introducing into the French woman's dialogue the words of Hersey—which are themselves the translated citation of a Japanese woman's eyewitness report—Duras makes possible the emergence, in the French woman's words, in her very claim to her own true vision of Hiroshima, of the insistence of another vision and another perspective, the perspective of the Japanese woman, whose experience of the catastrophe both is covered over and yet, in the dialogue of the lovers, persistently and uncannily returns.[28]

It is indeed the enigmatic language of untold stories—of experiences not yet completely grasped—that resonates, throughout the film, within the dialogue between the French woman and the Japanese man, and allows them to communicate, across the gap between their cultures and their experiences, precisely through what they do not directly comprehend. Their ability to speak and to listen in their passionate encounter does not rely, that is, on what they simply know of one another, but on what they do not fully know in their own traumatic pasts.

In a similar way, a new mode of seeing and of listening—a seeing and a listening *from the site of trauma*—is opened up to us as spectators of the film, and offered as the very possibility, in a catastrophic era, of a link between cultures. What we see and hear, in *Hiroshima mon amour*, resonates beyond what we can know and understand; but it is in the event of this incomprehension and in our departure from sense and understanding that our own witnessing may indeed begin to take place.[29]

3 TRAUMATIC DEPARTURES: SURVIVAL AND HISTORY IN FREUD

(*Beyond the Pleasure Principle, Moses and Monotheism*)

—*What happened?*
—*Happened?*
—*Yes.*
—*I didn't die.*

The Pawnbroker

In recent years, psychiatry, psychoanalysis, and neurobiology have increasingly insisted on the direct effects of external violence in psychic disorders. This trend has culminated in the study of *post-traumatic stress disorder*, or PTSD, which describes an overwhelming experience of sudden or catastrophic events in which the response to the event occurs in the often uncontrolled, repetitive appearance of hallucinations and other intrusive phenomena.[1] As it is generally understood today, post-traumatic stress disorder reflects the direct imposition on the mind of the unavoidable reality of horrific events, the taking over of the mind, psychically and neurobiologically, by an event that it cannot control. As such, PTSD seems to provide the most direct link between the psyche and external violence and to be the most destructive psychic disorder. I will argue in what follows that trauma is not simply an effect of destruction but also, fundamentally, an enigma of survival.[2] It is only by recognizing traumatic experience as a paradoxical relation between destructiveness and survival that we can also recognize the legacy of incomprehensibility at the heart of catastrophic experience.

The centrality and complexity of trauma in our century was first most profoundly addressed in two important and controversial works by Freud, *Beyond the Pleasure Principle* and *Moses and Monotheism*. These two pieces, written during the events surrounding World War I and World War II, respectively, have been called upon by contemporary critics as showing a direct relation between Freud's theory of trauma and historical violence, a directness presumably reflected in the theory of trauma he produces.[3] I will suggest that these two works, read together, represent Freud's formulation of trauma as a theory of the peculiar incomprehensibility of human survival. It is only by reading the theory of individual trauma in *Beyond the Pleasure Principle* in the context of the notion of historical trauma in *Moses and Monotheism* that we can understand the full complexity of the problem of survival at the heart of human experience.

▌ HISTORY AND SURVIVAL

Beyond the Pleasure Principle indeed opens with Freud's perplexed observation of a psychic disorder that appears to reflect the unavoidable and overwhelming imposition of historical events on the psyche. Faced with the striking occurrence of what were called the war neuroses in the wake of World War I, Freud is startled by the emergence of a pathological condition—the repetitive intrusion of nightmares and relivings of battlefield events—that is experienced like a neurotic pathology but whose symptoms seem to reflect, in startling directness and simplicity, nothing but the unmediated occurrence of violent events. Freud thus compares these symptoms to those of another long-problematic phenomenon, the accident neurosis. The reliving of the battle can be compared, he says, to the nightmare of an accident:

> Dreams occurring in traumatic neuroses have the characteristic of repeatedly bringing the patient back into the situation of his accident, a situation from which he wakes up in another fright. This astonishes people far too little. . . .
>   . . . Anyone who accepts it as something self-evident that their dreams should put them back at night into the situation that caused them to fall ill has misunderstood the nature of dreams. (13)[4]

The returning traumatic dream perplexes Freud because it cannot be understood in terms of any wish or unconscious meaning, but is, purely and inexplicably, the literal return of the event against the will of the one it inhabits. Unlike the symptoms of a normal neurosis, whose painful manifestations can be understood ultimately in terms of the attempted avoidance of unpleasurable conflict, the painful repetition of the flashback can only be understood as the absolute inability of the mind to avoid an unpleasurable event that has not been given psychic meaning in any way.[5] In trauma, that is, the outside has gone inside without any mediation. Taking this literal return of the past as a model for repetitive behavior in general, Freud ultimately argues, in *Beyond the Pleasure Principle*, that it is traumatic repetition, rather than the meaningful distortions of neurosis, that defines the shape of individual lives. Beginning with the example of the accident neurosis as a means of explaining individual histories, *Beyond the Pleasure Principle* ultimately asks what it would mean to understand history as the history of a trauma.

Freud's comparison of the war experience to that of the accident introduces another element as well, however, which adds to the significance of this question. For it is not just any event that creates a traumatic neurosis, Freud indicates, but specifically "severe mechanical concussions, railway disasters and other accidents involving a risk to life" (12). What Freud encounters in the traumatic neurosis is not the reaction to any horrible event but, rather, the peculiar and perplexing experience of survival. If the dreams and flashbacks of the traumatized thus engage Freud's interest, it is because they bear witness to a survival that exceeds the very claims and consciousness of the one who endures it. At the heart of Freud's rethinking of history in *Beyond the Pleasure Principle*, I would thus propose, is the urgent and unsettling question: *What does it mean to survive?*

A MISSED EXPERIENCE

The intricate relation between trauma and survival arises in this text, not, as one might expect, because of a seemingly direct and unmediated relation between consciousness and life-threatening events, but rather through the very paradoxical structure of *indirectness* in psychic trauma. Freud begins his discussion of trauma by noting the "bewildering" fact that psychological trauma does not occur in strict correspondence to the body's experience of a life threat, that is, through the wounding of the body; a bodily injury, Freud notes, in fact "works as a rule *against* the development of a neurosis" (12). Indeed, for consciousness, survival does not seem to be a matter of known experience at all. For if the return of the traumatizing event appears in many respects like a waking memory, it can nonetheless only occur in the mode of a symptom or a dream:

[People] think the fact that the traumatic experience is constantly forcing itself upon the patient even in his sleep is a proof of the strength of that experience: the patient is, as one might say, fixated to his trauma. . . .

I am not aware, however, that patients suffering from traumatic neurosis are much occupied in their waking lives with memories of their accident. Perhaps they are more concerned with *not* thinking of it. (13)

If a life threat to the body and the survival of this threat are experienced as the direct infliction and the healing of a wound, trauma is suffered in the psyche precisely, it would seem, because it is *not* directly available to experience.[6] The problem of survival, in trauma, thus emerges specifically as the question: What does it mean for *consciousness to survive*?

Freud's speculation on the causes of repetition compulsion in relation to the origins of consciousness can indeed by understood as an attempt to grasp the paradoxical relation between survival and consciousness. Freud suggests that the development of the mind seems, at first, to be very much like the development of the body: consciousness arises out of the need to protect the "little fragment of living substance . . . suspended in the middle of an external world charged with the most powerful energies," which "would be killed by the stimulation emanating from these if it were not provided with a protective shield against stimuli" (27). Unlike the body, however, the barrier of consciousness is a barrier of sensation and knowledge that protects the organism by placing stimulation within an ordered experience of time.[7] What causes, trauma, then, is a shock that appears to work very much like a bodily threat but is in fact a break in the mind's experience of time.

We may, I think, tentatively venture to regard the common traumatic neurosis as a consequence of an extensive breach being made in the protective shield against stimuli. This would seem to reinstate the old, naive theory of shock. . . . [It] regards the essence of the shock as being the direct damage to the molecular structure . . . of the nervous system, whereas what *we* seek to understand are the effects produced on the organ of the mind. . . . And we still attribute importance to the element of fright. It is caused by lack of any preparedness for anxiety. (31)

The breach in the mind—the conscious awareness of the threat to life—is not caused by a pure quantity of stimulus, Freud suggests, but by "fright," the lack of preparedness to take in a stimulus that comes too quickly. It is not simply, that is, the literal threatening of bodily life, but the fact that the threat is recognized as such by the mind *one moment too late.* The shock of the mind's relation to the threat of death is thus not the direct experience of the threat, but precisely the *missing* of this experience, the fact that, not being experienced *in time,* it has not yet been fully known.[8] And it is this lack of direct experience that, paradoxically, becomes the basis of the repetition of the nightmare:

> These dreams are endeavoring to master the stimulus retro-spectively, by developing the anxiety whose omission was the cause of the traumatic neurosis. (32)

The return of the traumatic experience in the dream is not the signal of the direct experience but, rather, of the attempt to overcome the fact that it was *not* direct, to attempt to master what was never fully grasped in the first place. Not having truly known the threat of death in the past, the survivor is forced, continually, to confront it over and over again. For consciousness then, the act of survival, as the experience of trauma, is the repeated confrontation with the necessity and impossibility of grasping the threat to one's own life. It is because the mind cannot confront the possibility of its death directly that survival becomes for the human being, paradoxically, an endless testimony to the impossibility of living. From this perspective, the survival of trauma is not the fortunate passage beyond a violent event, a passage that is accidentally interrupted by reminders of it, but rather the endless *inherent necessity* of repetition, which ultimately may lead to destruction.[9] The examples of repetition compulsion that Freud offers—the patient repeating painful events in analysis, the woman condemned repeatedly to marry men who die, the soldier Tancred in Tasso's poem wounding his beloved again[10]— all seem to point to the necessity by which consciousness, once faced with the possibility of its death, can do nothing but repeat the destructive event over and over again. Indeed, these examples suggest that the shape of individual lives, the history of the traumatized individual, is nothing other than the determined repetition of the event of destruction.

In modern trauma theory as well, there is an emphatic tendency to focus on the destructive repetition of the trauma that governs a person's life. As modern neurobiologists point out, the repetition of the traumatic experience in the flashback can itself be retraumatizing; if not life-threatening, it is at least threatening to the chemical structure of the brain and can ultimately lead to deterioration. And this would also seem to explain the high suicide rate of survivors, for example, survivors of Vietnam or of concentration camps, who commit suicide only *after* they have found themselves completely in safety. As a paradigm for the human experience that governs history, then, traumatic disorder is indeed the apparent struggle to die. The postulation of a drive to death, which Freud ultimately introduces in *Beyond the Pleasure Principle*, would seem only to recognize the reality of the destructive force that the violence of history imposes on the human psyche, the formation of history as the endless repetition of previous violence.

■ A TRAUMATIC AWAKENING

If we attend closely, however, to Freud's description of the traumatic nightmare of the accident, we find a somewhat more complex notion of what is missed, and repeated, in the trauma. In his description of the accident dream, Freud attributes the traumatic fright not simply to the dream itself, but to what happens upon waking up:

> Dreams occurring in traumatic neuroses have the characteristic of repeatedly bringing the patient back into the situation of his accident, a situation *from which he wakes up in another fright.*

If *fright* is the term by which Freud defines the traumatic effect of not having been prepared in time, then the trauma of the nightmare does not simply consist in the experience *within* the dream, but in *the experience of waking from it*. It is the experience of *waking into consciousness* that, peculiarly, is identified with the reliving of the trauma. And as such it is not only the dream that surprises consciousness but, indeed, the very *waking itself* that constitutes the surprise: the fact not only of the dream but of having passed beyond it. What is enigmatically suggested, that is, is that the trauma consists not only in having confronted death but in *having survived, precisely, without knowing it.* What one returns to in the flashback is not the incomprehensibility of one's near death, but the very incomprehensibility of one's own survival. Repetition, in other words, is not simply the attempt to grasp that one has almost died but, more fundamentally and enigmatically, the very attempt *to claim one's own survival.* If history is to be understood as the history of a trauma, it is a history that is experienced as the endless attempt to assume one's survival as one's own.

It is this incomprehensibility of survival, I would suggest, that is at the heart of Freud's formulation of the death drive. Freud describes the origin of the drive as a response to an awakening not unlike the awakening from a nightmare:

> The attributes of life were at some time awoken [*wurden . . . erweckt*] in inanimate matter by the action of a force of whose

nature we can form no conception. . . . The tension which then arose in what had hitherto been an inanimate substance endeavored to cancel itself out. In this way the first drive came into being: the drive to return to the inanimate state. (38, translation modified)

At the beginning of the drive, Freud suggests, is not the traumatic imposition of death but rather the traumatic "awakening" to life. Life itself, Freud says, is an awakening out of a 'death' for which there was no preparation. The origin of the drive is thus precisely the experience of having passed beyond death without knowing it. And it is in the attempt to master this awakening to life that the drive ultimately defines its historical structure: failing to return to the moment of its own act of living, the drive departs into the future of a human history.

DEPARTURE AND HISTORY

Indeed, it is the historical complexity of the story of departure and return that lies at the heart of Freud's most famous example of repetition compulsion, the game of the child playing *fort* and *da* with his spool.[11] Freud says that he observed the strange game of a child (his grandson) who repeatedly threw a wooden spool on a string into his cot, uttering the sound "o-o-o-o," then retrieved it, uttering "a-a-a-a." Freud interprets these sounds as meaning *fort*, "gone," and *da*, "here," and suggests that the child is reenacting the departure and return of his mother, which he had just recently been forced to confront.[12]

While Freud offers the game as part of his search for evidence of the repetition compulsion, what is most striking is not so much the meaning of the game itself, its exemplification or nonexemplification of repetition compulsion, as the way Freud presents the example, that is, his curious wavering, as the example unfolds, on the question whether the game is a game of departure or of return:

I eventually realized that it was a game and that the only use he made of any of his toys was to play "gone" with them.

This, then, was the complete game—disappearance and return. As a rule one only witnessed its first act, which was repeated untiringly as a game in itself, though there is no doubt that the greater pleasure was attached to the second act.

It may perhaps be said . . . that [his mother's] departure had to be enacted as a necessary preliminary to her joyful return, and that it was in the latter that lay the true purpose of the game. But against this must be counted the observed fact that the first act, that of departure, was staged as a game in itself and far more frequently than the episode in its entirety, with its pleasurable ending. (15–16)

What strikes Freud as he tells the story of the *fort-da* is that the game of departure and return is ultimately, and inexplicably, a game, simply, of departure.[13] I would suggest that if this game is resonant in *Beyond the Pleasure Principle*, it is not only because the child's play does or does not provide evidence of repetition compulsion. It is also because the symbolized pattern of departure and return brings into prominent view a larger conception of historical experience, a conception Freud was grappling with and trying to bring into focus in the writing of *Beyond the Pleasure Principle*.[14] This historical pattern, moreover, will be dealt with more explicitly in a later work that is also about the story of a departure and a return, the story of the history of the Jews in *Moses and Monotheism*. In the game of *fort-da*, that is, we already see what is implicit in the curious movement from the example of combat trauma to the death drive, the fact that the theory of trauma, as a historical experience of a survival exceeding the grasp of the one who survives, engages a notion of history exceeding individual bounds. To grasp the rethinking of individual trauma as an experience of departure, of a leaving behind of the event in *Beyond the Pleasure Principle*, means to have already arrived in the history—the collective, transgenerational, and religious history—of *Moses and Monotheism*.

In *Moses and Monotheism* Freud argues that the history of the Jews can be explained through the occurrence of a traumatic event, the murder of Moses during his return of the Hebrews from Egypt to Canaan. After the murder the Jews repressed it and took on a second leader, also named Moses, who was eventually assimilated to the first Moses, who had been murdered.[15] The belated experience of the murder and the return of the repressed Mosaic religion through Jewish tradition, Freud argues, ultimately established Jewish monotheism and determined the subsequent history of the Jews. A brief look at Freud's explanation of the history of the Jews in *Moses and Monotheism* will show how Freud's understanding of history as survival, in *Beyond the Pleasure Principle*, ultimately extends beyond the confines of the individual psyche and delineates the structure of Jewish historical experience.

■ HISTORICAL TRAUMA, OR THE HISTORY OF THE JEWS

The history of the Jews in *Moses and Monotheism* indeed resonates in significant ways with the theory of trauma in its attempt to understand the actual experience of the Jews—their historical development—in terms of an experience they cannot fully claim as their own, the passing on of the monotheistic religion. This passing on of monotheism is the experience of a determining force in their history that makes it not fully a history they have *chosen*, but precisely the sense of *being chosen by* God, the sense of chosenness that, Freud says, is what has enabled the Jews "to survive until our day."[16] Jewish monotheism, as the sense of chosenness, thus defines Jewish history around the link between survival and a traumatic history that exceeds their grasp.

The sense of chosenness, Freud argues, was originally taught to the Hebrews by Moses. But it was not truly part of a Jewish monotheistic religion, Freud suggests, until after Moses's death. As a consequence of the repression of the murder of Moses and of the return of the repressed that occurs after the murder, the sense of chosenness returns not as an object of knowledge but as an unconscious force, a force that manifests itself in what Freud calls "tradition." Thus Freud argues that the point of *Moses and Monotheism* is not to explain monotheism as a doctrine but rather to explain monotheism's peculiar *unconscious force* in shaping Jewish history:

> I have made all these psychological digressions to make it more credible that the religion of Moses exercised influence on the Jewish people *only when it had become a tradition.* (164; 127–28, emphasis added)

Arguing that monotheism is truly operative in Jewish history only as a "tradition," Freud suggests that the sense of being chosen is precisely *what cannot be grasped* in the Jewish past, the way in which its past has imposed itself upon it *as* a history that it survives but does not fully understand. Linking this formation of tradition to the traumatic murder of Moses, Freud implicitly argues that the structure of monotheism—the emergence, after the return of the repressed murder of Moses, of the sense of being incomprehensibly chosen by God to survive—is very similar, in certain respects, to the curious nature of the survival of trauma. Monotheism, in shaping Jewish history, turns out to function very much like what is described, in *Beyond the Pleasure Principle*, as the death drive. The question that governs the story of the individual in *Beyond the Pleasure Principle—What does it mean to survive?*—thus becomes, in the history of the Jews, the crucial and enigmatic query, *What does it mean to be chosen?*[17] The traumatic structure of monotheism at the heart of this question signifies a history of Jewish survival that is both an endless crisis and the endless possibility of a new future.

The argument that Freud presents is complex, but the basic problem that underlies the meaning of this question can be understood in terms of the nature of what it is, in the traumatic history of the Jews, that remains ungrasped and endlessly returning in the passing on of monotheism. On the one hand, Freud seems to suggest that what is central to Jewish history is the complex configuration of love, hatred, and loss that occurs during the traumatic murder of the father figure Moses. Using as his model the traumatic experience of the castration threat and its consequences in the development of the child, Freud suggests that the repression of the monotheistic religion following the murder of Moses and the subsequent return of his religion in tradition is like the repression and return of the repressed following the castration threat.[18] When the religion of Moses returns, it comes back in the form of an unconscious identification with the father.

Thus we might say, on the basis of the understanding of traumatic repetition that Freud outlines in *Beyond the Pleasure Principle*, that the murder of Moses, suffered as the traumatic separation from the father, ultimately leads to a belated attempt to return to the moment before the murder, to Moses's doctrine of chosenness. This attempt to return always confronts again the act of violence—the moment or cause of separation—in the form of later violence directed against the Jews: specifically, Freud argues, the Oedipal rivalry that others feel toward the Jews, most notably the rivalry and hatred of the Christians.[19] The separation from the father figure in the murder is thus an endlessly incomprehensible violence that is suffered, repeatedly, both as the attempt to return to the safety of chosenness and as the traumatic repetition of the violent separation, a return occurring through the violence imposed by the Christians. The history of chosenness, as the history of survival, thus takes the form of an unending confrontation with the returning violence of the past.[20]

THE POSSIBILITY OF A FUTURE

But we can understand the emergence and power of the Jewish sense of chosenness in monotheism in another way, an interpretation that is made possible by Freud's use, in the explanation of trauma in this text, not only of the model of Oedipal trauma but of the example, familiar from *Beyond the Pleasure Principle*, of the accident (an example discussed in chapter 1 above):

> It may happen that someone gets away, apparently unharmed, from the spot where he has suffered a shocking accident, for instance a train collision. In the course of the following weeks, however, he develops a series of grave psychical and motor symptoms, which can be ascribed only to his shock or whatever else happened at the time of the accident. He has developed a "traumatic neurosis." This appears quite incomprehensible and is therefore a novel fact. The time that elapsed between the accident and the first appearance of the symptoms is called the "incubation period". . . . As an afterthought we observe that—in spite of the fundamental difference in the two cases, the problem of the traumatic neurosis and that of Jewish monotheism—there is a correspondence in one point. It is the feature which one might term *latency*. There are the best grounds for thinking that in the history of the Jewish religion there is a long period, after the breaking away from the Moses religion, during which no trace is to be found of the monotheistic idea. . . . until . . . [tradition] . . . succeeded in waking to life the religion which Moses had instituted centuries before. (84; 67–68, translation modified)

In the occurrence of the accident, Freud seems to compare the traumatic history of the Jews, the breaking away from the Moses religion, to the murder of Moses and his return in the form of Jewish monotheism. But the event of the accident, as Freud describes it here, consists not only, as Freud puts it, in the "shock or whatever happened at the time of the accident" but also, we might argue, in the fact that the person "gets away, apparently unharmed." The leaving of the accident, that is, is not only the unexperienced event of the crash but the non-experiencing of the fact that the person has indeed remained "unharmed." I would propose that what returns in monotheism—the monotheistic idea that comes back after the latency of the Jewish people—is not simply the missed event of the violent separation but the incomprehensible sense, precisely, of having violently separated from Moses *and survived.* If monotheism for Freud is an "awakening," it is not simply a return of the past, but of the fact of having survived it, a survival that, in the figure of the new Jewish god, appears not as an act chosen by the Jews, but as the incomprehensible fact of *being chosen for* a future that remains, in its promise, yet to be understood. Chosenness is thus not simply a fact of the past but the experience of being shot into a future that is not entirely one's own. The belated experience of trauma in Jewish monotheism suggests that history is not only the passing on of a crisis but also the passing on of a survival that can only be possessed within a history larger than any single individual or any single generation.[21]

Freud's understanding of survival will only be fully grasped, I think, when we come to understand how it is through the peculiar and paradoxical complexity of survival that the theory of individual trauma contains within it the core of the trauma of a larger history.[22] One might perhaps, of course, attempt to understand Freud's own theory of trauma in *Beyond the Pleasure Principle* and in *Moses and Monotheism,* and his movement from one text to the next, through the many survivals and the suffering he was forced to face in World War I, World War II, and in between—the loss of his daughter Sophie, of his grandson, the threat to his son, and finally his forced departure from Vienna.[23] Rather than attempt such a task, however, I will point toward another kind of survival, one more like what Freud refers to in

Moses and Monotheism as the survival of "tradition": the survival Freud conceived as the very theory, the future tradition, of psychoanalysis. World War I, Freud believed, was less a threat to his life or his family than to psychoanalysis itself. And it is of psychoanalysis as a kind of survival that he writes in 1924 to Sandor Ferenczi:

> I have survived the Committee that was to have been my successor. Perhaps I shall survive the International Association. It is to be hoped that psychoanalysis will survive me. But it gives a somber end to one's own life.[24]

Freud suggests that psychoanalysis, if it lives on, will live on not as the straightforward life of a known and understood theory, but as the endless survival of what has not been fully understood. If psychoanalysis is to be continued in its tradition, it is paradoxically in what has not yet been fully grasped in its survival that its truest relation to its insight must be found. I would suggest that trauma theory is one of the areas today in which this survival is precisely taking place, not only in the assuredness of its transformation and appropriation by psychiatry but in the creative uncertainties of this theory that remain, for psychiatry *and* psychoanalysis, in the enigma of trauma as both destruction *and* survival, an enigma that lies at the very heart of the Freudian insight itself.

4 THE FALLING BODY AND THE IMPACT OF REFERENCE
(de Man, Kant, Kleist)

These puppets have the advantage of being antigravitational. They know nothing of the inertia of matter. . . . The puppets, like elves, need the ground only to brush it . . . we need it in order to rest, and to recover from the exertion of the dance.

Kleist, On the Marionette Theater

In the wake of structuralist and poststructuralist developments in literary theory, a good deal of concern has arisen that these linguistically oriented theories of reading deny the possibility that language can give us access to history. The constant focus by poststructuralists on the linguistic devices by which meaning is produced, and by "deconstruction" on the difficulties these devices create for our understanding of a text, seems to amount to a claim that language cannot refer adequately to the world and indeed may not truly refer to anything at all, leaving literature and language, and even consciousness in general, cut off from historical reality. Responding to this concern, Paul de Man states, in his 1982 essay "The Resistance to Theory," that linguistically oriented theories do not necessarily deny reference, but rather deny the possibility of modeling the principles of reference on those of natural law, or, we might say, of making reference like perception.[1] De Man's attempt to distinguish reference from natural law, which is tied to his understanding of the relation between constative and performative language, far from denying access to history, is a way, I will argue, of precisely keeping history from being swallowed up by the power of abstraction. This emphasis is to be read not only in de Man's statements about language, however, but most concretely in a story he repeatedly tells: the story, specifically, of a fall, not just of a figurative fall but also of a very literal falling. It is de Man's unexpected association of theory with falling that, I will suggest, constitutes the original insight of his theory, a theory that does not eliminate reference but precisely registers, in language, the impact of an event.

The essay "The Resistance to Theory" is a good framework for this inquiry because it is specifically about reference and it is also about falling. It begins by addressing the resistances, or objections, to theory made in the name of referential reality, or of an external world. It responds both by arguing conceptually for a resistance that stems from "within" theory and by associating this referential "resistance" with the additional connotation of something concrete, something like the resistance one feels upon impact, the impact, for example, one feels falling down. Those who resist theory in the name of perceptual reality, de Man seems to be arguing, are in fact resisting the force, or impact, of a fall.

A UNIVERSE OF FALLING

In order to understand de Man's argument we can turn to a narrative that is not explicitly articulated but can be read, I would suggest, in de Man's essay: the story of how the problem of reference became, in the history of thought, inextricably bound up with the fact of literal falling. This story emerges when de Man compares contemporary problems of reference to problems arising in the traditional philosophical project of linking the sciences of language (logic, rhetoric, and grammar) with the sciences of the world in general (arithmetic, geometry, astronomy, and music). The example de Man offers of such a project is seventeenth-century epistemology, which attempted to link language with mathematics through a logic comparable to analytical geometry, a geometry that articulated number with the phenomenal, spatial figures of curves and lines. The use of analytical geometry as a model for language exemplifies, de Man implies, the attempt to assimilate language to phenomenal reality.[2] But the example of seventeenth-century geometry as an ideal model of language bears special weight because the phenomenal world that this geometry seemed to describe so successfully was a world thought to be governed entirely by motion, a world whose phenomenal coherence *as* motion would come to an end toward the close of the seventeenth century. De Man appears to allude to this end when he follows the example of the philosophical ideal with the example of a literary text that this philosophy cannot account for, the title of Keats's poem "The Fall of Hyperion." For the world of simple motion was ended, once and for all, with the discovery, by Newton, of gravitational force, or the revolutionary notion, introduced in Newton's *Principia*, that objects fall toward each other. Newton suggested that the motions of massive bodies separated in space could be explained by an attractive force pulling them toward each other. It could be said, indeed, that with this assertion, the world of motion became, quite literally, a world of falling. I would suggest here that the history of philosophy after Newton could be thought of as a series of confrontations with the question of how to talk about falling. And similarly, the problem of reference, insofar as de Man implicitly associates it, in my interpretation, with this development in the history of philosophy, is: *how to refer to falling.*

If we step back for a moment, we can see how the problem of gravitation or universal falling could indeed be considered a problem of reference. Newton, in the story of his discovery of gravitation, sees an apple fall, and understands in a flash that the objects of the universe are all falling toward each other by the same force that pulls this apple, invisibly, toward the ground. Insofar as this notion was made by Newton into a law, or was represented by a *mathematical formula*, it allowed mathematical science to explain aspects of the world it had not been able to explain previously. But insofar as gravitation was also a concept, represented by a *word—gravity—*it remained philosophically incomprehensible, and seemed an "occult quality" or magical invisible entity that made no rational sense. That is, as a mathematical formula it could be applied perfectly to the world, but as a thing *referred* to by philosophical discourse it seemed a pure fiction.[3] Thus, with the introduction of gravitation, the only thing that was adequate to the world was, paradoxically, that which didn't refer (mathematics); and what did refer, language, could no longer describe the world. In a world of falling, reference could not adequately describe the world.

I would argue that de Man's allusion to this moment in the history of philosophy suggests that it is a paradigm for a problem that is central to contemporary theory: the recognition that direct or phenomenal reference to the world means, paradoxically, the production of a fiction; or otherwise put, that reference is radically different from physical law. Many of de Man's works indeed connect problems of theory with literary and philosophical scenes of falling,[4] but two in particular—his essay on Kant's *Critique of Judgment* and his essay on a story by Kleist, which also involves an implicit reading of Kant—can be seen as illuminating his arguments about theory, because Kant might be said to represent, in the history of philosophy, the attempt to deal rigorously with the referential problem by founding his theory on the very knowledge of its independence from empirical referents.[5]

In the following pages I will sketch briefly how de Man's readings of Kant and Kleist trace, first of all, the philosophical attempt to distinguish language from empirical law by making theory into a self-reflexive system. I will then show how de Man's reading also uncovers a resistance to this project arising within the language of philosophy that emerges in its use of examples, a referential resistance de Man will associate with a performative dimension of discourse. Both the necessity of theory and the resistance to it will occur, in de Man's analysis, in the transformation of a specific example—the example of falling—and through the appearance of a specific figure—the figure of a body. It is in de Man's insistence on the centrality of the body, I would suggest, that we can best understand how his own theory both conceptualizes and enacts a mode of referential resistance.

■ THE BODY OF PHILOSOPHY

De Man's introductory discussion of Kant focuses on the definition philosophy offers of itself, and the example by which it illustrates this definition. Kant defines philosophy by distinguishing what he calls "metaphysics"—basically, an expansion of Newton's laws of motion[6]—as an empirically determined set of laws, from the principles of pure or "transcendental" philosophy, which is entirely conceptual. Thus, empirical law tells us facts about the world, while transcendental philosophy tells us the conceptual conditions of possibility for thinking about the empirical world in the first place. The importance of this distinction, de Man tells us, is that it distinguished between an empirical discourse, which depends on given empirical facts, and a philosophical discourse, which is purely conceptual and hence does not depend on empirical givens. In other words, one might elaborate, pure philosophy defines itself as that which does not depend for its meaning on the empirical world; it knows itself *as* that which does not directly know the empirical object.

Just as significant as this conceptual distinction, however, is also, in de Man's analysis, the way in which philosophy uses an example—the example of bodies in motion—to define its conceptual purity. Kant illustrates the distinction between metaphysics and transcendental philosophy with the example of how each relates the phenomenon of bodies in motion to causality. Thus, for example, Kant says, a metaphysical law tells us that all changes in a moving body have an external cause (in Newtonian terms, all nonlinear motion is caused by external forces); the corresponding transcendental law tells us, rather, that all changes in bodies must have some cause. Remarking on this example, de Man notes its significance in relation to the definition of philosophy:

> The example of bodies in motion is . . . more than a mere example that could be replaced by any other; it is another version or definition of transcendental cognition. If critical philosophy and metaphysics . . . are causally linked to each other, their relationship is similar to the relationship, made explicit in the example, between bodies and their transformations or motions. (PMK, 123)

If philosophy gives up direct reference to the body in its definition of itself, it nonetheless reintroduces it, figuratively, in the example, which becomes a kind of implicit or secondary definition alongside the conceptual one. The body becomes in this secondary definition a figure for the very knowledge philosophy has about its inability to refer to bodies. Indeed, later in the essay de Man points to the appearance of an explicit bodily figure in Kant's description of the unified system of transcendental philosophy and metaphysics:

> That this unity is conceived in organic terms is apparent from the recurring metaphor of the body, as a totality of various limbs and parts ("*Glieder*," meaning member in all the senses of the word, as well as in the compound "*Gliedermann,*" the puppet of Kleist's Marionettentheater). (PMK, 142)

When the body reenters philosophy as a figure for its own knowledge, it is not only a moving body but a moving organic body, and ultimately a moving *human* body: a body that is a series of articulated parts. The human body, as a figure for a self-knowing philosophy, is also the figure for the knowledge of a difference: the difference between pure philosophy and empirical discourse. The possibility of a self-knowing, self-referential system of discourse—the paradigm of theory as the knowledge of its independence from empirical referents—is contained in its self-representation as a human body. Philosophy, or theory, incorporates its loss of reference to the falling empirical body into the conceptual gain of the presumably upright body of the philosophical system.

GRACEFUL FIGURES

The means by which philosophy would achieve this conceptual and linguistic freedom is suggested, in the lines quoted above, by de Man's surprising association of the limbs of the philosophical body—its *Glieder*—with the puppet—*Gliedermann*—of Kleist's story *On the Marionette Theater*. In this story, the acclaimed principal dancer of a local opera company admires the gracefulness of marionettes, which he claims to be superior to that of human dancers, and suggests that, indeed, a dancer who wanted to perfect his art "could learn a thing or two from them." The perfection is purely mechanical: merely by manipulating, with his strings, the puppet's center of gravity, the puppeteer creates in the limbs of the puppets the perfect curving motions of a dance, without the clumsiness of the human dancer, because in the puppets, the limbs are "what they should be: dead, mere pendula, governed only by the law of gravity." While this unsettling vision of swinging mechanical limbs surpassing human grace seems an unlikely comparison to the serious rationality of Kant's philosophical project, de Man's linking of the two suggests an uncanny similarity. Indeed, in an essay he wrote directly on Kleist's *Marionette Theater*, de Man suggests that the puppet dance can be read as the representation of a certain aesthetic model of self-knowledge in the tradition developing out of Kant.[7] De Man thus suggests that behind philosophy's own figure of its conceptual project, which would incorporate force, as an unknowable event, into the articulated body of philosophical thought, lies the ideal of a mechanism that lifelessly transforms the laws of force and motion into superhuman grace. The philosophical body, in other words, should not simply move upright, but dance: and dancing, its movements are no longer strictly human, but are rather the movements of lifeless, mechanical limbs. To understand Kant, de Man implies, is to grasp how the body of the system is both a human body and is at the same time the gracefully inhuman body of a marionette.

The superior gracefulness of the marionettes, de Man insists in the Kleist essay, lies specifically in the transformations that occur between the puppeteer and the puppet. The gracefulness of the puppet body is the result of the union between the mechanical puppet and the particular agency who directs:

> The puppets have no motion by themselves but only in relation to the motions of the puppeteer. . . . All their aesthetic charm stems from the transformations undergone by the linear motion

of the puppeteer as it becomes a dazzling display of curves and arabesques. . . . The aesthetic power is located neither in the puppet nor in the puppeteer but in the text that spins itself between them. (AFK, 285)

De Man suggests that the dance of the puppets represents a particular model of a written text, a text created by the relation between the puppeteer and the puppets. As de Man's essay continues, the relation between puppeteer and puppet, figured as the transformation of puppeteer-held strings into puppet motions, appears to represent the relation between the author and his writing. This, we may conjecture, is what de Man sees as a primary referential relation behind the text, and the beauty of the marionette dance is that it permits the difficulties of such referentiality to be lost, entirely, in a formal, quantified system that is as predictable, and ultimately nonspecific—or nonreferential—as a mathematics:

> This text is the transformational system, the anamorphosis of the line as it twists and turns into the tropes of ellipses, parabola, and hyperbole. Tropes are quantified systems of motion. The indeterminations of imitation and of hermeneutics have at last been formalized into a mathematics that no longer depends on role models or on semantic intentions. . . .
> Balanced motion compellingly leads to the privileged metaphor of a center of gravity. . . .
> On the other hand, it is said of the same puppets, almost in the same breath, that they are *antigrav* [antigravitational], that they can rise and leap, like Nijinsky, as if no such thing as gravity existed for them. . . . By falling (in all senses of the term, including the theological Fall) gracefully, one prepares the ascent, the turn from parabola to hyperbole, which is also a rebirth. (AFK, 285–86)

The exhilarating, graceful freedom of this movement lies in its elimination of any referential weight of a personal authorial self; the puppeteer is lost entirely in the movements of the puppets. The graceful image of the human body arises precisely, here, in the *loss* of any referential particularity. What makes this possible is indicated by de Man when he calls this a "transformational system" as well as a system of "tropes" or figures. For, as a transformational system, it is a grammar, a grammar conceived as a coded set of differences not based on any extralinguistic reality; what is at work here is the power of a grammar that incorporates referential differences into nonreferential, intralinguistic ones. Yet at the same time this loss of referential particularity appears, surprisingly, in the very figure of a human being. The paradox of this writing system is that it produces the human figure of the author in the very elimination of authorial referentiality. Precisely when the text appears most human, it is most mechanical. And this autobiographical paradox is also the philosophical paradox, de Man implicitly suggests, underlying Kant's bodily figure of philosophy: when philosophy conceives itself as a human form, it is in fact dependent on the workings of a purely formal grammar.

The appeal and tempting power of this formalization is indicated, moreover, in what happens, specifically, to falling. For in this system falling, as de Man remarks, is only a means of rising. And yet, if motion and force are easily assimilated by this system, de Man also notes a less easily assimilable element:

> One must . . . have felt some resistance to the unproblematic re-integration of the puppet's limbs and articulations, suspended in dead passivity, into the continuity of the dance. (AFK, 288)

The resistance one "must" have felt is not only a moral one but also the difficulty, arising within the formal system, of incorporating dead limbs into its phenomenal geometry, of turning death into life as falling was turned into rising.

Indeed, de Man points out that the dancer accompanies his

example of marionettes with an example that is less easily formalized:

> The passage is all the harder to assimilate since it has been preceded by the briskly told story of an English technician able to build such perfect mechanical legs that a mutilated man will be able to dance with them in Schiller-like perfection. . . . The dancing invalid in Kleist's story is one more victim in a long series of mutilated bodies that attend on the progress of enlightened self-knowledge. (AFK, 288–89)

In the context of de Man's reading of the marionette dance, this mutilated invalid can be nothing other than the reassertion of reference, which, from the perspective of the system, can appear only as a disruption and mutilation. Elsewhere in his essay, de Man makes it clear what figure, exactly, the dancing invalid comes to disrupt. It is the figure of the traditional autobiographical interpretation of Kleist:

> The received opinion is that, in this late work, Kleist achieves self-control and recovers a "naive form of heroism" by overcoming a series of crises and victories over "Todeserlebnisse" [death experiences] that can only be compared to as many deaths and resurrections. This is, of course, a very reassuring way to read *Marionettentheater* as a spiritual autobiography and . . . it is not entirely compatible with the complications of the tone and the diction. (AFK, 283)

The marionette dance, it turns out, describes the very reading by which critics have found the story to be Kleist's own spiritual autobiography. Believing they are finding, in *The Marionette Theater*, the moving human figure of Kleist himself, resurrected in his writing from the deaths of his experience, these critics have unknowingly described only the purely mechanical movements of a system that easily exchanges rising for falling, life for death, because all are equally free of referential weight. The dancing invalid disturbs this graceful yet mechanical illusion of autobiography with the suggestion of another, less formally recognizable life story.

■ A SHADOWY REALITY

De Man himself offers an alternative autobiographical reading in his essay, one that is, in contrast to the traditional spiritual biographies, somewhat more difficult to integrate:

> The only explicit referential mark in the text is the date of the action, given as the winter of 1801. Now 1801 is certainly an ominous moment in a brief life rich in ominous episodes. (AFK, 283)

In de Man's reading, the referential potential of the story thus seems to derive, not from the figure of the dance, but from what he will later call an "innocuous-looking notation," the innocuous number marking a date. If this date is to refer us to the referential Kleist, however, what we find most immediately is a series of crisis-ridden relations between Kleist and others with whose names he had come to be associated:

> 1801 . . . is the year when Kleist's self-doubts and hesitations about his vocation culminate in what biographers call his "Kant crisis." It is also the year during which Kleist's engagement to Wilhelmine von Zenge begins to falter and during which he is plagued by doubts similar to those which plagued Kierkegaard in his relationship to Regina and Kafka in his relationship to Felice. Between the two events, the Kant crisis and the forthcoming breach of promise with Wilhelmine (the final break occurred in the spring of 1802), there seems to be a connection which, if only he could understand it, would have relieved Kleist from his never resolved self-desperation. To uncover this link would be the ground of any autobiographical project. (AFK, 283–84)

As de Man reads Kleist's "life" from the notation "1801," he produces a series, not of movements, but of breaks, or rather of proper names that name particular discontinuities in the life: the crisis of reading Kant, the breach of promise with Wilhelmine, not to mention the introduction of several new proper names in the status of biographical analogues. The possibility of referential self-recognition becomes in de Man's story the possibility of providing a meaningful continuity between these breaks, a continuity presumably provided by the spiritual biographers when they speak of "death experiences" that will ultimately be redeemed through writing. The stakes of such autobiographical self-recognition are clear in de Man's reference to Kleist's self-desperation, which would eventually lead to a horrible suicide. But as de Man's story continues, Kleist's own attempts within his life to make meaningful links between events appear to be thwarted, precisely, in the bewildering displacements and substitutions that occur among the proper names attached to them, names that at times appear to take over the very reality of the unfortunate Kleist's life:

The link [between the Kant crisis and the break with Wilhelmine] actually and concretely existed in the reality of Kleist's history, but it took a somewhat circuitous route. For when Kleist next met his bride-to-be, in 1805 in Königsberg, she was no longer Fräulein Wilhelmine von Zenge but Frau Professor Wilhelmine von Krug. Dr. Wilhelm Traugott Krug was Kant's successor in the latter's chair in philosophy at the University of Königsberg. Kleist, who had wanted to be, in a sense, like Kant and who, one might conjecture, had to give up Wilhelmine in order to achieve this aim, found himself replaced, as husband, by Krug, who also, as teacher philosopher, replaced Kant. What could Kleist do but finish writing, in the same year 1805, a play to be called—what else could it have been—*Der zerbrochene Krug* [The broken Jug]?

All this, and much more, may have been retained, five more years later, in 1810, when he wrote *Über das Marionettentheater*, in the innocuous-looking notation: winter of 1801. (AFK, 284)

If there is indeed a link between the crises in Kleist's life, it is not one that Kleist could easily have grasped: where he apparently attempted to exchange one event for another—to gain Kant in his loss of Wilhelmine—he instead loses Kant *and Wilhelmine* precisely because *Wilhelm* gains them both. The figure for any Kleistian autobiography, de Man suggests, would thus be less appropriately the graceful and figurative falling and rising of dancing puppets than the smashed pieces of "the broken jug," a play that, incidentally, opens on the scene of a man who is injured from falling, not from falling figuratively, but from falling quite literally, and rather less exaltedly, out of bed. It would appear to be this unredeemable *literality* of the events of Kleist's life that emerges, then, in de Man's final insistence on the incomprehensible agency of the *letter* in Kleist's life:

> To decide whether Kleist knew his text to be autobiographical or pure fiction is like deciding whether or not Kleist's destiny, as a person and as a writer, was sealed by the fact that a certain doctor of philosophy happened to bear the ridiculous name of Krug. A story that has so many K's in it (Kant, Kleist, Krug, Kierkegaard, Kafka, K) is bound to be suspicious no matter how one interprets it. Not even Kleist could have dominated such randomly overdetermined confusion. (AFK, 284)

Read alongside the dancer's story of the marionettes, de Man's story of numbers and names, and their simultaneous connection and dispersal through names and letters, reveals a break, a mutilated limb, perhaps, in the continuity of the abstract, formal, philosophical dance of Kleist's traditional biographers. The proliferation of letters in de Man's story is less a denial of reference, indeed, than the active assertion of a literality, the disruption of any so-called autobiographical reading that would, in perceiving behind Kleist's writing the figurative face of his past, in fact reduce his referential specificity to a mere figure. It is paradoxically only through such a disruption, through such "randomly overdetermined confusion," or through the interruption of the marionettes by the falling of a broken body, de Man strikingly implies, that a shadowy autobiographical reality first begins to emerge.[8]

■ THE IMPACT OF REFERENCE

In the essay on Kant, similarly, de Man remarks on a break within the system, a system that also, as in the puppet theater, models itself as a formal articulation of phenomenal motions deflected by forces. The break occurs in Kant's text precisely in the attempt to integrate force into the system of motions. In his analysis of Kant, de Man identifies this break specifically as a disruption in the phenomenal self-representation of language, or in the appearance in language of a performative dimension:

> From the pseudo-cognition of tropes, language has to expand to the activity of performance. . . . The *Critique of Judgment* therefore has, at its center, a deep, perhaps fatal, break or discontinuity. It depends on a linguistic structure (language as a performative as well as a cognitive system) that is not itself accessible to the powers of transcendental philosophy. (PMK, 131–32)

Knowing itself as a grammar or a system of tropes, philosophy must, and yet cannot, fully integrate a dimension of language that not only shows, or represents, but acts. Designating this moment as "fatal," de Man associates it, as in the Kleist story, with death. It is paradoxically in this deathlike break, or resistance to phenomenal knowledge, that the system will encounter the resistance, de Man suggests, of reference.

Indeed, just at that point in the *Critique of Judgment* where the figure of force is being integrated into the body of philosophy, de Man locates an oddly unassimilable model of reflection:

the model of a vision, not exactly a perception, that is not aimed at the unification of the whole, but is rather a vision of individual parts. This model is accompanied, again, by an example, the example of the human body, not, however, as a unified whole but as a system of nonpurposive parts, parts seen, as Kant says, "without regard for the purposes which all our limbs serve." As de Man remarks, this example reflects on the self-knowledge of the philosophical system; but in this case we no longer perceive a unity, but read a kind of disarticulation:

> We must, in short, consider our limbs, hands, toes, breasts, or what Montaigne cheerfully referred to as "Monsieur ma partie" [Mister Member], in themselves, severed from the organic unity of the body. . . . We must, in other words, disarticulate, mutilate the body in a way that is much closer to Kleist than to Winckelmann, though close enough to the violent end that happened to befall both of them. (PMK, 142)

In de Man's reading of this example the body does not represent philosophy figuratively as the *formalization of number,* but rather comes to have, in the list of individual body parts, the *force of enumeration.* This force disarticulates the system as it attempts to distinguish and unify empirical and conceptual discourse, that is, to know itself as independent of empirical referents. The disarticulation of the body is thus not something known or stated by philosophy, but something that occurs in its attempt to free itself from reference. While this can only appear, from the perspective of philosophy, as a mutilation, such mutilation also designates the reassertion of a referential moment, a referentiality that is not, however, to be understood within the phenomenal, formalizable opposition of empirical and conceptual knowledge. In terms of the example, we could say that while the force of enumeration mutilates the body as a whole, it at the same time establishes, in this disarticulation of limbs, or naming of parts, the very specificity of a human, as opposed to puppet, body. The reappearance, through de Man's reading, of a body, though mutilated, is thus the paradoxical evocation of a referential reality neither fictionalized by direct reference nor formalized into a theoretical abstraction.[9]

We can only recognize such a referential force, however, if we take into account what happens in de Man's own text when he, like Kant before him, introduces an example; that is, when he compares the mutilation we "must" do in reading Kant to two very specific deaths, the "violent end" that "happened to befall" Kleist and Winckelmann. The names of Kleist and Winckelmann here—two prominent writers in the German aesthetic tradition—are not figures for their thoughts or writing, but are rather attached to the specificity of the two men's actual deaths: the death of Kleist, who, following a suicide pact contracted with Henriette Vogel, shot first her and then himself with a gun; the death of Winckelmann who, on the other hand, was murdered in Trieste, for a couple of gold coins, by an Italian named Arcangeli. The particularity of this double example is itself a referential moment in de Man's text, but it is not, however, a referentiality we can subsume or understand in either a purely conceptual, or in a purely phenomenal, way. Indeed, it is an example of the occurrence of a difference: the difference between living and dying—which resists being generalized into a conceptual or figural law. This is the difference that, we recall, appeared in, but remained unassimilable to, the formal system, a difference it could not know, just as, we could add, the system was unable to know the event of falling. And this is also what de Man's text does not know when it refers to Kleist's and Winckelmann's deaths as something that "befalls" them; when it names, that is, a befalling. In de Man's text, as in Kant's, the impact of reference is felt in falling: in the resistance of the *example of falling* to a phenomenal or perceptual analogy that would turn it into the mere figure of an abstract principle. In naming a befalling, de Man's text no longer simply knows what it says, but indeed does more than it knows, and it is in this that we can read the referential significance of his own theory.

This significance has the weight of a paradox: that reference emerges not in its accessibility to perception, but in the resistance of language to perceptual analogies; that the impact of reference is felt, not in the search for an external referent, but in the necessity, and failure, of theory. This theoretical knowledge, however, cannot be separated from the particular performance of de Man's own text, which always accompanies its theoretical lesson with a story. It is the originality and unique referential resonance of de Man's writing, I would suggest, to discover the resistance of theory in the story it tells of its own falling. What theory does, de Man tells us repeatedly, is fall; and in falling, it refers. To capture the reality of this falling is the crucial task de Man's theoretical work is engaged in, and it is the task that falls upon us as we read the very particular story of de Man's writing.

5 TRAUMATIC AWAKENINGS

(Freud, Lacan, and the Ethics of Memory)

Les désirs entretiennent les rêves. Mais la mort, elle, est du côté du réveil.

Jacques Lacan

Ever since its emergence at the turn of the century in the work of Freud and Pierre Janet, the notion of trauma has confronted us not only with a simple pathology but also with a fundamental enigma concerning the psyche's relation to reality. In its general definition, trauma is described as the response to an unexpected or overwhelming violent event or events that are not fully grasped as they occur, but return later in repeated flashbacks, nightmares, and other repetitive phenomena. Traumatic experience, beyond the psychological dimension of suffering it involves, suggests a certain paradox: that the most direct seeing of a violent event may occur as an absolute inability to know it; that immediacy, paradoxically, may take the form of belatedness. The repetitions of the traumatic event—which remain unavailable to consciousness but intrude repeatedly on sight—thus suggest a larger relation to the event that extends beyond what can simply be seen or what can be known, and is inextricably tied up with the belatedness and incomprehensibility that remain at the heart of this repetitive seeing.

In the present chapter I propose to study the problem of seeing and knowing as it appears in a dream told by Freud—the dream of a father who has lost his child and who dreams about this child in the night that follows the child's death—and in the reinterpretation of this dream by Jacques Lacan in his seminar "Tuché and Automaton."[1] While Freud introduces the dream in *The Interpretation of Dreams* as an exemplary (if enigmatic) explanation of why we sleep—how we don't adequately face the death outside of us—Lacan suggests that already at the heart of this example is the core of what would later become, in *Beyond the Pleasure Principle*, Freud's notion of traumatic repetition, and especially the traumatic nightmares that, as Freud says, "wake the dreamer up in another fright." In Lacan's analysis, Freud's dream is no longer about a father sleeping in the face of an external death, but about the way in which, in his traumatic awakening, the very identity of the father, as subject, is bound up with, or founded in, the death that he survives. What the father cannot grasp in the death of his child, that is, becomes the foundation of his very identity as father. In thus relating trauma to the very identity of the self and to one's relation to another, Lacan's reading shows us, I will suggest, that the shock of traumatic sight reveals at the heart of human subjectivity not so much an epistemological, but rather what can be defined as an *ethical* relation to the real.

■ THE STORY OF A DREAM

At the beginning of the seventh chapter of *The Interpretation of Dreams* Freud introduces a surprising dream that links his theory of dreams and wish-fulfillment to the question of external reality, and specifically to a reality of death, catastrophe, and loss. Freud narrates the dream as follows:

A father had been watching beside his child's sick-bed for days and nights on end. After the child had died, he went into the next room to lie down, but left the door open so that he could see from his bedroom into the room in which his child's body was laid out, with tall candles standing round it. An old man had been engaged to keep watch over it, and sat beside the body murmuring prayers. After a few hours' sleep, the father had a dream that *his child was standing beside his bed, caught him by the arm and whispered to him reproachfully: "Father, don't you see I'm burning?"* He woke up, noticed a bright glare of light from the next room, hurried into it and found that the old watchman had dropped off to sleep and that the wrappings and one of the arms of his beloved child's dead body had been burned by a lighted candle that had fallen on them.

The explanation of this moving dream is simple enough. . . . The glare of light shone through the open door into the sleeping man's eyes and led him to the conclusion which he would have arrived at if he had been awake, namely that a candle had fallen over and set something alight in the neighbourhood of the body. It is even possible that he had felt some concern when he went to sleep as to whether the old man might not be incompetent to carry out his task.

. . . the words spoken by the child must have been made up of words which he had actually spoken in his lifetime and which were connected with important events in the father's mind. For instance, '*I'm burning*' may have been spoken during the fever of the child's last illness, and '*Father, don't you see?*' may have been derived from some other highly emotional situation of which we are in ignorance.

But, having recognized that the dream was a process with a meaning, and that it can be inserted into the chain of the dreamer's psychical experiences, we may still wonder why it was that a dream occurred at all in such circumstances, when the most rapid possible awakening was called for. (5:509–10)[2]

Unlike in other dreams, Freud remarks, what is striking in this dream is not its relation to inner wishes, but its direct relation to a catastrophic reality outside: the dream takes its "moving" power, it would seem, from the very simplicity and directness of its reference, the burning of his child's body that the father sees through his sleep. Seeing the light through his closed eyes, the father comes to the conclusion that he would have come to if he had been awake, that the candle has fallen onto the body of his child. Yet the very directness of this dream, Freud remarks, does not, surprisingly, wake the father and permit him to rush to save the burning corpse, but rather *delays* his response to the waking reality. If the meaning and reference of the dream are indeed clear, Freud suggests, then it is not apparent why they should appear at all *in a dream*, that is, in a form that delays the father's response—a response that is urgently called for—to the reality to which it points. Precisely because the dream is so direct, and because the reality to which it refers is so urgent in its demand for attention, this dream poses the question: In the context of a violent reality, *why dream rather than wake up?*

Freud first attempts to answer this question by referring the dream to the theory of wish-fulfillment, in spite of its direct representation of the child's unwished-for death. For while the dream points to the horrible reality of the child's burning, it does so, Freud suggests, precisely by transforming the dead child into a living one. The dream fulfills, therefore, the father's wish that the child be still alive:

Here we shall observe that this dream, too, contained the fulfilment of a wish. The dead child behaved in the dream like a living one: he himself warned his father, came to his bed, and caught him by the arm, just as he had probably done on the occasion from the memory of which the first part of the child's words in the dream were derived. For the sake of the fulfilment of this wish the father prolonged his sleep by one moment. The dream was preferred to a waking reflection because it was able to show the child as once more alive. If the father had woken up first and then made the inference that led him to go into the next room, he would, as it were, have shortened his child's life by that moment of time. (5:509)

While the dream seems to show the reality of the burning outside, it in fact hides, Freud suggests, the reality of the child's death. The dream thus transforms death into life and does this, paradoxically, with the very words that refer to the reality of the burning. It is in order to fulfill the wish to see the child alive, in other words, that the knowledge of his child's burning is turned into a dream. If the father dreams rather than wakes up, it is because he cannot face the knowledge of the child's death while he is awake. It is thus not so much that the father simply "doesn't see" the burning corpse ("Father, don't you see")—he does see it—but rather that he cannot see it and be awake at the same time. For the father, Freud seems to imply, the knowledge of the death of his child can perhaps appear only in the form of a fiction or a dream.[3] The dream thus tells the story of a father's grief as the very relation of the psyche to reality: the dream, as a delay, reveals the ineradicable gap between the reality of a death and the desire that cannot overcome it except in the fiction of a dream.

CONSCIOUSNESS AND SLEEP

After completing his original analysis, however, Freud remains unsatisfied with the explanation and returns to the dream again at a later point in the chapter, where the problem of the dream's delay of awakening comes back to take on new meaning. For the interpretation of the dream as the fulfillment of the father's wish leads to a deeper question that concerns not only this singular instance but the way in which the father may represent the very nature of consciousness itself:

> Let me recall the dream dreamt by the man who was led to infer from the glare of light coming out of the next room that his child's body might be on fire. The father drew this inference in a dream instead of allowing himself to be woken up by the glare; and we have suggested that one of the psychical forces responsible for this result was a wish which prolonged by that one moment the life of the child whom he pictured in the dream. . . . we may assume that a further motive force in the production of the dream was the father's need to sleep; his sleep, like the child's life, was prolonged by one moment by the dream. "Let the dream go on"—such was his motive—"or I shall have to wake up." In every other dream, just as in this one, the wish to sleep lends its support to the unconscious wish. (5:570–71)

The wish in the father's dream to keep the child alive—the first reason Freud gives for the father's dream—is inextricably bound up, it turns out, with a more profound and enigmatic wish, the father's wish to sleep. This wish is enigmatic because, as Freud suggests, it comes not only from the body but from consciousness itself, which desires somehow its own suspension. And this wish, moreover, is not limited to this single father, exhausted by his task of watching over the child, but indeed refers to a desire common to all sleepers. The dream of the burning child does not simply represent, therefore, the wish-fulfillment of a single father, tired and wishing to see his child alive once again; but, more profoundly and more enigmatically, the wish fulfillment of consciousness itself:

> All dreams . . . serve the purpose of prolonging sleep instead of waking up. *The dream is the GUARDIAN of sleep* and not its disturber. . . .

Thus the wish to sleep (which the conscious ego is concentrated upon
. . .) must in every case be reckoned as one of the motives for the for-
mation of dreams, and every successful dream is a fulfilment of that
wish. (4:233–34, translation modified)

The specific wish behind the dream of the burning child, the
wish to see the child again, Freud suggests, like the wish behind
any dream, is tied to a more basic desire, the desire of consciousness as such *not to wake up.* It is not the father alone who
dreams to avoid his child's death, but *consciousness itself* that, in
its sleep, is tied to a death from which it turns away. It is not primarily the wish to keep the child alive that motivates the father's
sleep but rather the wish of consciousness to sleep that—even
at the expense of a burning reality—motivates the dream. The
dream is thus no longer simply linked to a wish within the
unconscious fantasy world of the psyche; it is rather, Freud
seems to suggest, *something in reality itself that makes us sleep.* The
question concerning the father—*Why dream rather than wake
up?*—thus ultimately becomes, in Freud's analysis, a more profound and mysterious question concerning consciousness itself:
What does it mean to sleep? And what does it mean to wish to sleep?

▮ THE STORY OF AN AWAKENING

Freud's analysis of the dream, and its implicit question in *The
Interpretation of Dreams*, seems to leave us with the sense of a
consciousness not only tied up with but also blinded to a violent
reality outside. But when Lacan turns to the dream in his seminar, he suggests that the question of sleep and Freud's analysis
of it contain within them, implicitly, another question, a question discovered not through the story of the father's sleep but
rather through the story of how and why the father wakes up:

> You will remember the unfortunate father who went to rest in
> the room next to the one in which his dead child lay—leaving
> the child in the care, we are told, of another old man—and who

is awoken by something. By what? It is not only the reality, the shock, the knocking, a noise made to recall him to the real, but this expresses, in his dream, the quasi-identity of what is happening, the very reality of an overturned candle setting light to the bed in which his child lies.

Such an example hardly seems to confirm Freud's thesis in the *Traumdeutung*—that the dream is the realization of a desire.

What we see emerging here, almost for the first time, in the *Traumdeutung*, is a function of the dream of an apparently secondary kind—in this case, the dream satisfies only the need to prolong sleep. What, then, does Freud mean by placing, at this point, this particular dream, stressing that it is in itself full confirmation of his thesis regarding dreams?

If the function of the dream is to prolong sleep, if the dream, after all, may come so near to the reality that causes it, can we not say that it might correspond to this reality without emerging from sleep? After all, there is such a thing as somnambulistic activity. The question that arises, and which indeed all Freud's previous indications allow us here to produce, is—*What is it that wakes the sleeper?* Is it not, *in* the dream, another reality?—the reality that Freud describes thus—*Dass das Kind an seinem Bette steht*, that the child is near his bed, *ihn am Arme fasst*, takes him by the arm and whispers to him reproachfully, *und ihm vorwurfsvoll zuraunt: Vater, siehst du denn nicht*, Father, don't you see, *dass ich verbrenne*, that I am burning?

Is there not more reality in this message than in the noise by which the father also identifies the strange reality of what is happening in the room next door? (57–58)[4]

In explaining the dream as fulfilling the wish to sleep, Lacan suggests, Freud implicitly points toward the fact that this wish is enigmatically defied in waking up; for if consciousness as such is what desires not to wake up, the waking is in conflict with the conscious wish. But what is particularly striking for Lacan is that this contradiction of the wish to sleep does not come simply from the outside, from the noise or light of the falling candle,

but from the way in which the words of the child themselves
bear precisely upon sleeping and waking. In Lacan's analysis,
indeed, the words of the child, "Father, don't you see I'm burning?" do not simply represent the burning without, but rather
address the father from within, and appeal to him as a complaint
about the very fact of his own sleep. It is *the dream itself*, that is,
that wakes the sleeper, and it is in this paradoxical awakening—an
awakening not to, but against, the very wishes of consciousness—that the dreamer confronts the reality of a death from
which he cannot turn away. If Freud, in other words, suggests
that the dream keeps the father asleep, Lacan suggests that it is
because the father dreams, paradoxically enough, that he precisely wakes up. The dream thus becomes, in Lacan's analysis,
no longer a function of sleep, but rather a function of awakening. If Freud asks, *What does it mean to sleep?* Lacan discovers at
the heart of this question another one, perhaps even more urgent: *What does it mean to awaken?*

ENCOUNTERING THE REAL

It might seem that Lacan, in his focus on awakening, moves
from the fictional dream world of Freud—the fictional world of
the child once again alive—to the simple reality of the external
world, the accident of the candle falling on the body, which re-
duplicates and underscores the reality of the child's death. But
what can Lacan mean by saying that the father is awoken not
simply by the sound of the candle's fall, but rather by the words
of the child *within* the dream? What does it mean, in other
words, that the father's dream achieves not the desired resusci-
tation of the child, but the dreamer's awakening to the child's
death? Indeed, to the extent that the father is awakened by the
dream itself, his awakening to death is not a simple movement
of knowledge or perception but rather, Lacan seems to suggest,
a paradoxical attempt *to respond, in awakening, to a call that can
only be heard within sleep.*

I would propose that it is in this paradoxical awakening by the dream itself that Lacan discovers and extends the specific meaning of the confrontation with death that is contained within Freud's notion of trauma.[5] For if the dreamer's awakening can be seen as a response to the words, to the address of the child, within the dream, then the awakening represents a paradox about the necessity and impossibility of confronting death. As a response to the child's request, the plea to be seen, the father's awakening represents not only a responding, that is, but a missing, a bond to the child that is built upon the impossibility of a proper response. Waking up in order to see, the father discovers that he has once again *seen too late* to prevent the burning. The relation between the burning within and the burning without is thus neither a fiction (as in Freud's interpretation) nor a direct representation, but a *repetition* that reveals, in its temporal contradiction, how the very bond of the father to the child—his responsiveness to the child's words—is linked to the missing of the child's death. To awaken is thus precisely to awaken only to one's repetition of a previous failure to see in time. The force of the trauma is not the death alone, that is, but the fact that, in his very attachment to the child, the father was unable to witness the child's dying as it occurred. *Awakening, in Lacan's reading of the dream, is itself the site of a trauma,* the trauma of the necessity and impossibility of responding to another's death.[6]

THE NATURE OF SURVIVAL

From this perspective, the trauma that the dream, as an awakening, reenacts is not only the missed encounter with the child's death but also the way in which that missing also constitutes the very survival of the father. His survival must no longer be understood, in other words, merely as an accidental living beyond the child, but rather as a mode of existence determined by the impossible structure of the response. By shifting the cause of the awakening from the accident of the candle falling outside the dream to the words of the child inside the dream, that is, Lacan suggests that the awakening itself is not a simple accident, but engages a larger question of responsibility.

In rethinking the meaning of the accident and linking it to this question about the nature of survival, Lacan is drawing here, I would propose, on Freud's late work on trauma, and specifically, on Freud's emphasis on the accident nightmare in *Beyond the Pleasure Principle* and on the example of the train accident in Freud's last major work, *Moses and Monotheism*.[7] Freud shows here how the traumatic accident—the confrontation with death—takes place too soon, too suddenly, too unexpectedly, to be fully grasped by consciousness. In Lacan's text, this peculiar accidentality at the heart of Freud's notion of trauma is linked to the larger philosophical significance of traumatic repetition:

> Is it not remarkable that, at the origin of the analytic experience, the real should have presented itself in the form of that which is *unassimilable* in it—in the form of the trauma, determining all that follows, and imposing on it an apparently accidental origin? (55)

Likewise, in the awakening of the father from the dream, the gap between the accident of the burning outside and the words of the child in the dream produces a significance greater than any chance awakening out of sleep, a significance that must be read in the relation between the chance event and the words it calls up:

> Between what occurs as if by chance, when everybody is asleep—the candle that overturns and the sheets that catch fire, the meaningless event, the accident, the piece of bad luck—and the poignancy, however veiled, in the words *Father, don't you see I'm burning*—there is the same relation to what we were dealing with in repetition. It is what, for us, is represented in the term neurosis of destiny or neurosis of failure. (69)

If the awakening reenacts the father's survival of his son's death, then this survival is no longer simply the effect of an accident but carries within it, and is defined by, its response to the words of the dead child.

It is this determining link between the child's death and the father's survival that constitutes, I would propose, Lacan's central discovery in the dream and his profound insight into its analysis by Freud: if Freud reads in the dream of the burning child the story of a sleeping consciousness figured by a father unable to face the accidental death of his child, Lacan, for his part, reads in the awakening the story of the way father *and* child are inextricably bound together through the story of a trauma. Lacan, in other words, reads the story of the father as a survival inherently and constitutively bound up with the address of a dead child.

The father's story of survival is, therefore, no longer simply his own, but tells, as a mode of response, the story of the dead child. This story itself has a double dimension: depending on whether the child's words are read as referring to the burning within or to the burning without, the father's survival can be understood, as we shall see, in terms of two inextricably bound, though incompatible, responses to the child's address. In thus implicitly exploring consciousness as figured by the survivor whose life is inextricably linked to the death he witnesses, Lacan resituates the psyche's relation to the real not as a simple matter of seeing or of knowing the nature of empirical events, not as what can be known or what cannot be known about reality, but as the story of an urgent responsibility, or what Lacan defines, in this conjunction, as an *ethical* relation to the real.[9]

A FAILED ADDRESS

If the words of the child—*Father, don't you see I'm burning?*—can be read, in this light, as a plea by the child to see the burning *within* the dream, the response of the father in this awakening dramatizes, as I have suggested, the story of a repeated *failure* to respond adequately, a failure to see the child in its death. For to see the child's living vulnerability as it dies, the father has to go on dreaming. In awakening, he sees the child's death too late, and thus cannot truly or adequately respond.

From this perspective, the dream reveals, indeed, a reality beyond the accident of a single empirical event, the chance death of a child by fever. For showing, in its repetition, the failure of the father to see even when he tries to see, the dream reveals how the very consciousness of the father as father, as the one who wishes to see his child alive again so much that he sleeps in spite of the burning corpse, is linked inextricably to the impossibility of adequately responding to the plea of the child in its death. The bond to the child, the sense of responsibility, is in its essence tied to the impossibility of recognizing the child in its potential death. And it is this bond that the dream reveals, exemplarily, as the real, as an encounter with a real established around an inherent impossibility:

> What encounter can there be henceforth with that forever inert being—even now being devoured by the flames—if not the encounter that occurs precisely at the moment when, by accident, as if by chance, the flames come to meet him? Where is the reality in this accident, if not that it repeats something actually more fatal *by means of* reality, a reality in which the person who was supposed to be watching over the body still remains asleep, even when the father reemerges after having woken up? (58)

In his awakening, the father's response repeats in one act a double failure of seeing: a failure to see adequately inside and a failure to see adequately outside.

Indeed, Lacan's interpretive movement from the accident of the candle falling to the dream as what repeats something "more fatal" by means of reality could be said to represent a parable about the notions of reality and trauma in Freud's late work, and specifically a parable about the movement from chapter 4 to chapter 5 of *Beyond the Pleasure Principle*. In this work, Freud indeed moves from a speculation on consciousness that explains trauma as an interruption of consciousness by something, such as an accident, that comes too soon to be expected, to an explanation of the origins of life itself as an "awakening" from death that precisely establishes the foundation of the drive and of consciousness alike.[10] This peculiar movement therefore traces a significant itinerary in Freud's thought from trauma as an exception, an accident that takes consciousness by surprise and thus disrupts it, to trauma as the very origin of consciousness and all of life itself. This global theoretical itinerary is revisited in Lacan's interpretation of the dream of the burning child, in his suggestion that the accidental in trauma is also a revelation of a basic, ethical dilemma at the heart of consciousness itself insofar as it is essentially related to death, and particularly to the death of others.[11] Ultimately, then, the story of father and child is, for Lacan, the story of an impossible responsibility of consciousness in its own originating relation to others, and specifically to the deaths of others. As an awakening, the ethical relation to the real is the revelation of this impossible demand at the heart of human consciousness.[12]

AN UNAVOIDABLE IMPERATIVE

But the words of the child, "Father, don't you see I'm burning?" can be read another way as well, not only as the plea to see the child burning in the dream but also as the command to see the child burning without, as the imperative, that is, to awaken. While Lacan does not explicitly articulate this reading, he does suggest that the missing of the trauma is also an encounter:

For what we have in the discovery of psycho-analysis is an encounter, an essential encounter—an appointment to which we
are always called with a real that eludes us. (53)

From this perspective, the awakening embodies an appointment
with the real. The awakening, in other words, occurs not merely
as a failure to respond but as an enactment of the inevitability
of responding: the inevitability of awakening to the survival of
the child that is now only a corpse. The pathos and significance
of this awakening derive not simply from the repeated loss of
the child, in the father's attempt to see, but rather from the fact
that it is the child itself—the child whom the father has not seen
in time, the child he has let die unwitnessed, the child whom the
dream (in the father's desperation to make the child live again)
shows as once again alive—it is this child who, from within the
failure of the father's seeing, commands the father to awaken and
to live, and to live precisely as the seeing of another, a different
burning. The father, who would have stayed inside the dream
to see his child alive once more, is commanded by this child to
see not from the inside—the inside of the dream, and the inside
of the death, which is the only place the child could now be truly
seen—but from the outside, to leave the child in the dream so
as to awaken elsewhere. It is precisely the dead child, the child
in its irreducible inaccessibility and otherness, who says to the
father: *wake up, leave me, survive; survive to tell the story of my
burning.*

To awaken is thus to bear the imperative to survive: to survive no longer simply as the father of a child, but as the one who
must tell *what it means not to see,* which is also what it means to
hear the unthinkable words of the dying child:

Is not the dream essentially, one might say, an act of homage to
the missed reality—the reality that can no longer produce itself

except by repeating itself endlessly, in some never attained awakening? (58)

Only a rite, an endlessly repeated act, can commemorate this not very memorable encounter—for no one can say what the death of a child is, except the father *qua* father, that is to say, no conscious being. (59)

The father must receive the dead child's words. But the only way truly to hear is now by listening not as a living father listens to a living child, but as the one who receives the very gap between the other's death and his own life, the one who, in awakening, does not see but enacts the impact of the very difference between death and life. The awakening, in its very inability to see, is thus the true reception of an address that, precisely in its crossing from the burning within to the burning without, changes and reforms the nature of the addressee around the blindness of the imperative itself. For in awakening, in responding to the address of the dead child, "Father, don't you see I'm burning?" the father is no longer the father of a living child, but precisely now the father as *the one who can say* what the death of a child is. The father's response to the address is not a knowing, that is, but an awakening; an awakening that, like the performance of a speaking, carries with it and transmits the child's otherness, the father's encounter with the otherness of the dead child.

Such an awakening, if it is in some sense still a repetition of the trauma (a reenactment of the child's dying), is not, however, a simple repetition of the *same* failure and loss—of the story of the father alone—but a new act that repeats precisely a departure and a difference: the departure of the father at the command of his burning child, and the difference to which he awakens, the intolerable difference between the burning within and the burning without.

As an act, the awakening is thus not an understanding but a transmission, the performance of an act of awakening that contains within it its own difference—"Repetition," Lacan says, "demands the new" (61). This newness is enacted in the fact that the words are no longer mastered or possessed by the one who says them—by the child who has died and for whom it is eternally too late to speak, or by the father who receives the words as coming from the place of the child, the self that was asleep. Neither the possession of the father nor the possession of the child, the words are *passed on* as an act that does not precisely awaken the self but, rather, *passes the awakening on to others.*

The accident is thus not a reality that can simply be known once and for all, but an encounter with the real that must take place each time anew in the accident of where the words happen to fall:

> But what, then, was this accident? When everybody is asleep, including the person who wished to take a little rest, the person who was unable to maintain his vigil and the person of whom some well intentioned individual, standing at his bedside, must have said, *He looks just as if he is asleep,* when we know only one thing about him, and that is that, in this entirely sleeping world, only the voice is heard, *Father, don't you see I'm burning?* This sentence is itself a firebrand—of itself it brings fire where it falls— and one cannot see what is burning, for the flames blind us to the fact that the fire bears on the *Unterlegt,* on the *Untertragen,* on the real. (59)

The accident, the force of the falling of the candle, is not confinable simply to a real that consists in the empirical fact of burning, or the fever, the accident by which the child caught fever or by which the candle fell and set the body of the child on fire while the father slept. The force of the fall lies precisely in the accident of the way in which the child's words transmit a burning that turns between the death of the child and the imperative of the father's survival, a burning that, like the candle, falls to awaken, anew, those who hear the words.

■ "I, TOO, HAVE SEEN"

The implications of such a transmission will only be fully grasped, I think, when we come to understand how, through the act of survival, the repeated failure to have seen in time—in itself a pure repetition compulsion, a repeated nightmare—can be transformed into the imperative of a speaking that awakens others. For now, however, I will simply point to the imperative of awakening that underlies Lacan's own text, the theoretical text of psychoanalysis. For it is in the language of theory itself, Lacan suggests, that psychoanalysis transmits, as he puts it, the "fever" of Freud, the burning of Freud's driving question, "What is the first encounter, the real, that lies behind the fantasy?" (54). And it is to this burning question, and to this fever that he senses in Freud's text, that Lacan's own text precisely responds:

> The function of . . . the real as encounter—the encounter in so far as it may be missed, in so far as it is essentially the missed encounter—first presented itself in the history of psychoanalysis in a form that was in itself already enough to *awaken* our attention, that of the trauma. (55, emphasis added)

Lacan suggests that the inspiration of his own text is awakened by the theory of trauma at the center of Freud's text, and that the Freudian theory of trauma speaks already (in this story of the burning dream and of the burning child) from within the very theory of wish-fulfillment. The passing on of psychoanalytic theory, Lacan suggests, is an imperative to awaken that turns between a traumatic repetition and the ethical burden of a survival.[13] It is, indeed, not simply Freud's perception and analysis of a reality outside or inside (the reality of empirical events or of internal "fantasies") that Lacan transmits in his reading of the Freudian text and in his concept of "the real," but rather, most importantly, what Lacan refers to as the "ethical witness" of Freud.[14] The Freudian text, Lacan seems to be telling us, is the site of a trauma, a trauma that appears to be located in the impact of the theory of trauma on psychoanalytic dream theory itself.

In the third part of "Tuché and Automaton," Lacan attempts to read, indeed, another moment in Freud's text—a moment where, in his late theory of trauma, Freud examines a phenomenon that once again implicates a child. In discussing the general phenomenon of traumatic repetition, Freud moves from the example of the nightmares of the soldiers who have come back from the war, to the repetition he observes in a child's game: the game of saying, alternately, *fort* and *da* while throwing a wooden spool back and forth, which symbolizes, in Freud's reading, the departure of the mother and the child's anxiety that she might not return. Freud's biographers have taught us that this game was in fact played by Freud's own grandchild; it was indeed the son of Freud's own daughter, Sophie, who was, through this game, coping with the suffering of the possible protracted absence or loss of his mother, by repeating or reenacting her departure. "It is the repetition of the mother's departure," Lacan says, "as cause of a *Spaltung* [splitting] in the subject—overcome by the alternating game, *fort-da*" (62–63). The trauma of the parent's departure, Lacan suggests, is thus relived in the traumatic experience of the child.[15]

But we also know that it was Freud himself who, as a father, lost his child, his daughter Sophie, to a fever—to pneumonia—a death at which he was unable to be present. It is thus particularly striking, I would suggest, that at this specific point in his text Lacan himself interrupts his analysis of the *fort-da* game with a voice that is itself, in turn, autobiographical. Following his commentary on the child's *fort-da* game, Lacan interjects into his own text—his own rethinking of the Freudian theory of trauma—a personal memory and a personal analogy. While Lacan, in this reminiscence, is literally positioned as the father, it is unclear whether his pathos resonates from the perspective of the father or from the perspective of the child. In his seminar, before the audience of his students and his trainees, Lacan thus testifies:

> I, too, have seen, seen with my own eyes, opened by maternal divination, the child, traumatized by the fact that I was going away despite the appeal, precociously adumbrated in its voice, and henceforth more renewed for months at a time—long after, having picked up this child—I have seen it let its head fall on my shoulder and drop off to sleep, sleep alone being capable of giving him access to the living signifier that I had become since the date of the trauma. (63, translation modified)

With the description of his own recollection of the trauma of his child, Lacan seems to suggest that the child inherits, in effect, the traumatic lapse, or absence, of the father. But with his emphasis on the significance of sleep as an enigma, and with the words "I, too, have seen," Lacan implies that his own text has passed on another Freudian story, the story of the father impelled to see by the dream of his dying child. Indeed, while he sees "with [his] own eyes," the father does not, in effect, see, and does not see as an ordinary father; for his eyes, he says, have needed to be "opened"—"opened," as he puts it, "by maternal divination." As a father, Jacques Lacan himself does not precisely see, but rather passes, once again, from an act of seeing-too-late, a not-seeing of the traumatized child, to a revelationlike *opening* of his own eyes by another, who has thus produced in him, precisely, an awakening; an awakening that engages less the past than the unknown future of the bond between the father and the child.

THE TRANSMISSION OF PSYCHOANALYSIS

Indeed, in his theoretical and autobiographical repetition of Freud's story, Lacan could not possibly have known that his text on trauma, like Freud's, in effect anticipated his own crucial loss and trauma: for it would be some years after this seminar that Lacan himself, like Freud, would survive the death of his own child, Caroline, who would be killed in a car accident.[16] What Lacan passes on in his moving retelling of the dream once told by Freud, even while he is in part unaware of its full reality for his own future, is the testimony to the tragedy of the father's survival: his survival of a child who unexpectedly dies before her father in an accident. Quite uncannily, Lacan's life will repeat Freud's loss of his own daughter Sophie to a fever, a disaster that was, at the time of writing, the unknown future of *Beyond the Pleasure Principle*. Lacan's transmission of the future of Freud's text on repetition, and, in general, the passing on of psychoanalytic writing, does not consist in the knowledge of a death that could simply be seen, but in the transmission of, precisely, an act of awakening. In opening the other's eyes, the awakening consists not in seeing but in handing over the seeing it does not and cannot contain to another (and another future).

The transmission of the psychoanalytic theory of trauma, the story of dreams and of dying children, cannot be reduced, that is, to a simple mastery of facts and cannot be located in a simple knowledge or cognition, a knowledge that can see and situate precisely where the trauma lies. In Lacan's text, as in Freud's, it is rather the words of the child that are ultimately passed on— passed on not merely from son to father but from daughter to "maternal divination." What is passed on, finally, is not just the meaning of the words but their performance: a performance that, in Lacan's text, takes place in the movement—in the repetition and the gap—between the German, from which these words address the future, and the French, in which they are received:

Qu'est-ce qui réveille? N'est-ce pas, *dans* le rêve, une autre réalité?—cette réalité que Freud nous décrit ainsi—*Dass das Kind an seinem Bette steht*, que l'enfant est près de son lit, *ihn am Arme fasst*, le prend par le bras, et lui murmure sur un ton de reproche, *und ihm vorwurfsvoll zuraunt: Vater, siehst du denn nicht,* Père, ne vois-tu pas, *dass ich verbrenne?* que je brûle?[17]

The passing on of the child's words transmits not simply <u>a reality that can be grasped in these words' representation</u>, but the <u>ethical imperative of an awakening that has yet to occur.</u>

∎ NOTES

INTRODUCTION: THE WOUND AND THE VOICE

1. Sigmund Freud, *Beyond the Pleasure Principle*, in *The Standard Edition of the Complete Psychological Works of Sigmund Freud*, translated from the German under the general editorship of James Strachey in collaboration with Anna Freud, assisted by Alix Strachey and Alan Tyson, 24 vols. (London: Hogarth, 1953–74), vol. 18, ch. 3 (hereafter cited as *SE*).

2. In the three original languages of the various literary and psychoanalytic texts analyzed in this book the terms are, respectively, *trauma* (English), *Trauma* (German), and *traumatisme* and *trauma* (French).

3. Jean Laplanche describes the temporal structure of trauma in the early texts of Freud in his classic book *Vie et mort en psychanalyse* (Paris: Flammarion, 1970), published in English as *Life and Death in Psycho-*

analysis, trans. Jeffrey Mehlman (Baltimore: Johns Hopkins University Press, 1976). A more general view of the problem can be found in his "Notes on Afterwardsness," in *Jean Laplanche: Seduction, Translation, Drives*, a dossier edited by John Fletcher and Martin Stanton (London: Institute of Contemporary Arts, 1992). In his other writings on trauma in Freud, Laplanche underscores the way in which Freud places the temporal story alongside a spatial one that is not spatial in the physical sense but rather about "extension" (see his *Problématiques I, L'angoisse* [Paris: PUF, 1980], 216–29, and "Traumatisme, traduction, transfert et autres trans(es)," in *La révolution copernicienne inachevée: Travaux, 1967–1992* [Paris: Aubier, 1992]). It is this double structure that also seems to be linked to the possibility of memorialization; Jacques Derrida suggests that in Freud a topographical structure is essential to the possibility of an archive (as the possibility of memory) (see Jacques Derrida, *Mal d'archive: Une impression freudienne* [Paris: Galilée, 1995]). The example of Tasso's story seems to demonstrate both the temporal and the spatial aspects of the notion of trauma.

4. It is instructive to recall, in this connection, the beautifully articulated notion of a temporal crisis in the introduction to Carol Jacobs's *Telling Time: Lévi-Strauss, Ford, Lessing, Benjamin, de Man, Wordsworth, Rilke* (Baltimore: Johns Hopkins University Press, 1994): "Time is what their narratives are about—not necessarily as subject matter but as the condition of the possibility of telling and as the crisis that it endures." For an important rethinking of temporality and experience in relation to catastrophe, see Maurice Blanchot, *L'écriture du désastre* (Paris: Gallimard, 1980), published in English as *The Writing of Disaster*, trans. Ann Smock (Lincoln: University of Nebraska Press, 1986).

5. It is through this recurrence of the example of the accident and the irreducibility of the literary story attached to it that I would also attempt to address the problem, central to the study of trauma, of its specificity or uniqueness. For on the one hand, the very notion of trauma as what comes unexpectedly suggests that traumatic stories convey the event that exceeds or is an exception to experience as such. Yet on the other hand, the notion of trauma as that which most clearly marks the past, and its structural description as a delayed experience, may lead to a seemingly universalizing description in which experience itself becomes tied up with trauma. In *Beyond the Pleasure Principle*, indeed, Freud begins with the example of a battle and a life-threatening accident, which are exceptions to ordinary experience, but ends up by

describing the origins of consciousness and of life and the drive in terms structurally parallel to those he has used to describe traumatic experience. And in my own studies in chapters 2, 3, and 4, I link the notion of trauma to a larger conception of the very "possibility of history." Yet the movement to origins in Freud or my own language of possibility is not, I would argue, an attempt to identify experience with trauma but rather an attempt to allow, within experience, for the very unexpected interruption of experience constituted by the traumatic accident. For to define trauma as simply that which comes from outside, rather than as a possibility inscribed within experience, would be, essentially, to make a claim for the possibility of defining, and thus anticipating, the difference between experience and trauma: to be able to categorize, to name, and thus, theoretically, to anticipate the accident. It is rather the notion of the traumatic possibility inscribed in human experience, a possibility always there but never certain, that transmits what is most accidental in, and hence unique to, its actual occurrence. The question concerning the specificity of trauma can be observed in the debates about the definition of trauma in the American Psychiatric Association's *Diagnostic and Statistical Manual of Mental Disorders*, which defines trauma both in terms of the specific types of events that cause it (the controversial "category a") and in terms of symptomatic responses, which are not explicitly tied to specific kinds of events. On this problem see my introduction to part 1 of *Trauma: Explorations in Memory*, ed. Cathy Caruth (Baltimore: Johns Hopkins University Press, 1995), as well as Laura Brown's essay in that volume, "Not Outside the Range: One Feminist Perspective on Psychic Trauma."

6. The return of the flashback as an interruption—as something with a disrupting force or impact—suggests that it cannot be thought simply as a representation. The rethinking of reference in nonrepresentational terms (or more accurately in terms of an interruption of a representational mode) in de Man, which I examine in chapter 4, is thus closely linked to my study, in chapter 5, of Lacan's speculation on trauma as a "waking" rather than a "seeing," a theory that I connect implicitly to the notion of the performative.

7. Saul Friedlander, in a chapter called "Trauma and Transference" in *Memory, History, and the Extermination of the Jews of Europe* (Bloomington: Indiana University Press, 1993), raises the question, in part in relation to my work on *Moses and Monotheism*, whether traumatic repetition allows for more positive ways of thinking through the possibil-

ity of history. This touches on the difficult question whether the flashback or repetition, as long as it remains unassimilable to consciousness,
can be considered truly historical. I would suggest that it might be possible to distinguish between the notion of referentiality and historicity
in this case; the return of the event could then be considered referential but not historically experienced. The historical experience, which
would involve the story of survival and thus the possibility of passing
on to another (or memorializing), would perhaps have to engage, then,
in addition, some notion of address or of the possibility of address.
Thus the chapters on *Hiroshima mon amour* and Lacan's reading of the
dream of the burning child try to grapple with what it means for a traumatic return not only to remain a flashback but to awaken the survivor
and to awaken the survivor to an address.

The question of memorializing through one's death or one's life, or
memorializing an event through the relation between death and life, is
perhaps linked to another question, the question of what it is that one
means to recall (a life or a death). On this question, see James Young,
The Texture of Memory: Holocaust Memorials and Meaning (New Haven;
Yale University Press, 1993); Geoffrey Hartman, "Learning from Survivors: The Yale Testimony Project," *Holocaust and Genocide Studies* 9,
no. 2 (1995); and Nadine Fresco, "Remembering the Unknown," *International Review of Psychoanalysis* 11 (1984).

8. The impact of trauma, the Tasso example thus suggests, is transmitted in psychoanalytic theory not only because traumatic experience
has there been explained or fully understood but also because the encounter with trauma has transformed and estranged the very language
of psychoanalytic writing. Indeed, as I suggest, if the story of the wound
offers a parable of traumatic experience, it also serves, in its staging of
the figure of the wound, as a parable of the very term *trauma*, of the
complexity of the very discourse, that is, of Freud's theoretical (or spec-
ulative) language. For the story of the movement from the original
wounding of Clorinda to the wounding of the tree can also be read as
the story of the emergence of the meaning of trauma from its bodily
referent to its psychic extension (see n. 3 above, and Laplanche's work
cited there). And as such, the Tasso example suggests that the language
of trauma does not simply originate in a theoretical knowledge that
stands outside of trauma but may emerge equally from within its very
experience. Yet this inner link between the experience of trauma and
its theory, or between the language of survivors and the language of

theoretical description, need not imply a lack of objectivity or truth, but the very possibility of speaking from within a crisis that cannot simply be known or assimilated.

The relation between language and trauma is examined from a clinical perspective in numerous discussions of language and trauma that struggle with the role of language in the therapeutic treatment of trauma. Most of these discussions suggest that the treatment of trauma requires the incorporation of trauma into a meaningful (and thus sensible) story. This would presumably extend to the theorization of trauma stemming from the therapeutic work (see, for example, Jodie Wigren, "Narrative Completion in the Treatment of Trauma," *Psychotherapy* 31, no. 3 [1994]). I am suggesting here, and throughout this book, the possibility of another way of thinking, or rethinking, this relation between trauma and language.

An interesting perspective on the examination of the impact of trauma on language was offered at the Wellfleet seminar in 1993 (lead by Robert Jay Lifton), where it was suggested by the scholar Ashis Nandy that the problem of witnessing trauma as a professional is learning the difficult task of speaking of trauma in the terms offered by the survivor.

The implication of the theory of trauma in its own object, or the inextricability of the theory from what it describes, could be indirectly linked to the insistence of some writers on the fact that the history of trauma theory—its repeated emergences and disappearances—looks a lot like the phenomenon of traumatic recall itself. See, for example, Elizabeth A. Brett and Robert Ostroff, "Imagery and Posttraumatic Stress Disorder: An Overview," *American Journal of Psychiatry* 142 (1985); and Judith Herman, *Trauma and Recovery* (New York: Basic Books, 1992).

CHAPTER I UNCLAIMED EXPERIENCE

1. For a recent expression of this opinion, see S. P. Mohanty, "Us and Them," *Yale Journal of Criticism* 2, no. 2 (1989).

2. There is no firm definition for *trauma*, which has been given various descriptions at various times and under different names. For a good discussion of the history of the notion and for recent attempts to define it, see Charles R. Figley, ed., *Trauma and Its Wake*, 2 vols. (New York: Brunner-Mazel, 1985–86).

3. Freud to Zweig, 30 May 1934, in *The Letters of Sigmund Freud and*

Arnold Zweig, ed. Ernst L. Freud (New York: Harcourt Brace Jovanovich, 1970).

4. While in the context of Jewish history the term *exile* refers, strictly speaking, to the exile in Babylon, the Egyptian captivity was considered paradigmatic of this later event. Thus *The Encyclopedia of Judaism* says, under the heading "exile," that "it is this 'prenatal' Egyptian servitude which becomes the paradigm of *Galut* [exile] in the rabbinic mind" (see Geoffrey Wigoder, *The Encyclopedia of Judaism* [New York: Macmillan, 1989]).

5. *Created* is an accurate translation of the German text, which reads, "hat . . . geschaffen."

6. Among the more interesting attempts to grapple with the political dimension of *Moses and Monotheism* are Jean-Joseph Goux, "Freud et la structure religieuse du nazisme," in his *Les Iconoclastes* (Paris: Seuil, 1978); and Philippe Lacoue-Labarthe et Jean-Luc Nancy, "Le peuple juif ne rêve pas," and Jean-Pierre Winter, "Psychanalyse de l'antisémitisme," both in *La Psychanalyse est-elle une histoire juive?* ed. Adelie Rassiel et Jean-Jacques Rassiel (Paris: Seuil, 1981).

7. It is interesting to note that this future can also be thought of in terms of the divine offer of a "promised land," and thus can be understood in terms of the future-oriented temporality of the promise.

8. Quotations from *Moses and Monotheism* are followed by two sets of page numbers. The first set refers to Sigmund Freud, *Moses and Monotheism,* trans. Katherine Jones (New York: Vintage Books, 1939), which I use in this essay; the second set refers to James Strachey's translation of *Moses and Monotheism* in *SE,* vol. 23.

9. See Edwin R. Wallace, "The Psychodynamic Determinants of *Moses and Monotheism,*" *Psychiatry* 40 (1977). There is a long history of psychoanalytic interpretations of Freud's writing on Moses. Among the more interesting are Marthe Robert, *D'Oedipe à Moïse: Freud et la conscience juive* (Paris: Calmann-Levy, 1974), published in English as *From Oedipus to Moses: Freud's Jewish Identity,* trans. Ralph Manheim (London: Routledge & Kegan Paul, 1977); and Marie Balmary, *Psychoanalyzing Psychoanalysis,* trans. Ned Luckacher (Baltimore: Johns Hopkins University Press, 1982). A review and critique of the applied psychoanalytic tradition in this context is to be found in Yosef Hayim Yerushalmi's excellent study of Moses and Monotheism, *Freud's Moses: Judaism Terminable and Interminable* (New Haven: Yale University Press, 1991).

10. There are, of course, a number of exceptions to this standard interpretation. Among them are Goux, "Freud et la structure religieuse du nazisme"; Lacoue-Labarthe and Nancy, "Le peuple juif ne rêve pas"; Winter, "Psychanalyse de l'antisémitisme"; Yerushalmi, *Freud's Moses*, cited above, as well as Ritchie Robertson, "Freud's Testament: *Moses and Monotheism*," in *Freud in Exile*, ed. Edward Timms and Naomi Segal (New Haven: Yale University Press, 1988); and Michel de Certeau's excellent essay "The Fiction of History: The Writing of *Moses and Monotheism*," in his *Writing of History* (New York: Columbia University Press, 1988). Useful treatments of Freud and Judaism include Yerushalmi, *Freud's Moses*; Philip Rieff, *The Mind of the Moralist* (New York: Anchor Books, 1961); and Martin S. Bergmann, "Moses and the Evolution of Freud's Jewish Identity," *Israel Annals of Psychiatry and Related Disciplines* 14 (March 1976). A useful bibliography can be found in Peter Gay, *Freud: A Life for Our Time* (New York: Doubleday, 1988); Gay's own discussion in this work of Freud's Jewish identity and of the writing of *Moses and Monotheism* is highly illuminating.

11. It is also interesting that the two vehicles, coming together, seem to resemble the two men named Moses and the two people coming together, in a missing meeting, at Qadeš. Freud describes this event also as a kind of gap: "I think we are justified in separating the two people from each other and in assuming that the Egyptian Moses never was in Qadeš and had never heard the name of Jahve, whereas the Midianite Moses never set foot in Egypt and knew nothing of Aton. In order to make the two people into one, tradition or legend had to bring the Egyptian Moses to Midian; and we have seen that more than one explanation was given for it" (49; 41).

The significance of *Moses and Monotheism* as a renewal of some of Freud's earliest thinking on trauma is indicated by his use of the figure of the "incubation period" to describe traumatic latency; Freud had used this figure in his early writing in *Studies on Hysteria* (1895) (see *SE*, vol. 2).

12. It is important to note that Freud does not imply the necessity of any particular kind of persecution; that is, while he insists on what appears to be a kind of universality of trauma, he does not suggest that the response to trauma must necessarily be the mistreatment of the

other. In fact, he distinguishes Christian hatred of the Jews from Nazi persecution, describing the former as determined by an Oedipal structure, while of the latter he says, "We must not forget that all the peoples who now excel in the practice of anti-Semitism became Christians only in relatively recent times, sometimes forced to it by bloody compulsion. One might say that they all are 'badly christened'; under the thin veneer of Christianity they have remained what their ancestors were, barbarically polytheistic. They have not yet overcome their grudge against the new religion which was forced on them, and they have projected it on the source from which Christianity came to them. . . . The hatred for Judaism is at bottom hatred for Christianity, and it is not surprising that in the German National Socialist revolution this close connection of the two monotheistic religions finds such clear expression in the hostile treatment of both" (117; 91–92). A brilliant exploration of the relation between Judaism and Christianity in the work of five authors, which takes off from the question of return in the story of Abraham, can be found in Jill Robbins, *Prodigal Son and Elder Brother: Augustine, Petrach, Kierkegaard, Kafka, Levinas* (Chicago: University of Chicago Press, 1991).

13. German quotations of *Moses and Monotheism* are taken from Sigmund Freud, *Studienausgabe*, band 9 (Frankfurt am Main: Fischer Wissenschaft, 1982).

14. What is translated here as "As an afterthought" is *nachträglich* in German, the word Freud uses elsewhere to describe the "deferred action" or retroactive meaning of traumatic events in psychic life; here what is *nachträglich* is Freud's theoretical insight, which thus also participates in the traumatic structure. An excellent discussion of the structure and temporality of trauma in early Freud can be found in Cynthia Chase, "Oedipal Textuality," in *Decomposing Figures: Rhetorical Readings in the Romantic Tradition* (Baltimore: Johns Hopkins University Press, 1986); and in Jean Laplanche, "Sexuality and the Vital Order," in Laplanche, *Life and Death in Psychoanalysis*.

15. Freud to Ernst Freud, 12 May 1938, in *Letters of Sigmund Freud*, ed. Ernst L. Freud, trans. Tania Stern and James Stern (New York: Basic Books, 1960).

16. The resonance of the letter to Ernst with *Moses and Monotheism*

is also apparent in the lines that follow those quoted above: "I some-times compare myself with the old Jacob who, when a very old man, was taken by this children to Egypt, as Thomas Mann is to describe in his next novel. Let us hope that it won't also be followed by an exodus from Egypt. It is high time that Ahasuerus came to rest somewhere." For the context of this writing see Peter Gay's excellent final chapter of *Freud: A Life for Our Time,* "To Die in Freedom," which first alerted me to the letter.

17. Robert Jay Lifton's marvelous treatment of trauma in Freud, in "Survivor Experience and Traumatic Syndrome," in his *Broken Connection: On Death and the Continuity of Life* (1979; New York: Basic Books, 1983), points to the relation between the later development of the notion of trauma and the occurrence of World War I. It would be interesting to explore how the notion of trauma inscribes the impact of war in Freud's theoretical work.

CHAPTER 2 LITERATURE AND THE ENACTMENT OF MEMORY

1. This chapter draws on both the filmic and the textual version of *Hiroshima mon amour.* Quotations in English are from Marguerite Duras and Alain Resnais, *Hiroshima mon amour,* trans. Richard Seaver (New York: Grove Press, 1961); quotations in French are from *Hiroshima mon amour* (Paris: Gallimard, 1960).

2. See James Monaco, *Alain Resnais* (New York: Oxford University Press, 1979).

3. On the complex relation between the visual images of the film and the spoken words, see Anne-Marie Gronhovd and William C. Vanderwolk, "Memory as Ontological Disruption: *Hiroshima mon amour* as a Postmodern Work," in *In Language and in Love: Marguerite Duras: The Unspeakable, Essays for Marguerite Duras,* ed. Mechthild Cranston (Potomac, Md.: Scripta Humanistica, 1992); and Marie-Claire Ropars-Wuilleumier, "Film Reader of the Text," *Diacritics,* spring 1985.

4. In the context of the comments concerning the end of the war in *Hiroshima mon amour,* it is interesting to note the last line of *Nuit et brouillard:* "Et il y a nous qui regardons sincèrement ces ruines comme si le vieux monstre concentrationnaire était mort sous les décombres, qui feignons de reprendre espoir devant cette image qui s'éloigne, comme si on guérissait de la peste concentrationnaire, nous qui

122 Notes to Pages 29–36

feignons de croire que tout cela est d'un seul temps et d'un seul pays, et qui ne pensons pas à regarder autour de nous, et qui n'entendons pas qu'on crie sans fin" [And there are those of us who sincerely regard these ruins as if the old concentration-camp monster were dead under the ashes, who pretend to be hopeful before this image that moves away, as if one could be cured of the concentration-camp plague, we who pretend to believe that all of this is of one time and of one country, and who don't think to look around us, and who don't hear the endless cry].

5. For an analysis of the structure of reference, see chapter 4.

6. The pathos of this necessity is expressed by Guy Lecouvette: "On découvre . . . qu'elle [l'oeuvre de Resnais] repose sur un pivot: la nécessité d'oublier pour vivre et la peur de l'oublier" [One discovers . . . that the work of Resnais rests on one pivot: the necessity of forgetting in order to live, and the fear of forgetting]. (In "Alain Resnais ou le souvenir," *L'Avant-scène du Cinéma*, February 1961).

7. *Raisonnable*—the word that describes what the woman had so long tried to refuse, in order to be faithful to the memory of her beloved—resonates interestingly with Resnais's use of it to describe the narrative form that he refuses in both this film and a later one: "Il y a dans ces deux films [*Hiroshima mon amour* and *L'année dernière à Marienbad*] le refus d'un récit chronologique où les événements sont présentés dans un ordre en apparence raisonnable" [There is in these two films the refusal of a chronological narrative where the events are presented in an order that appears reasonable]. See the interview conducted by Yvonne Baby in *Le Monde*, 29 August 1961.

8. The resonance between the complexity of "liberation" in the woman's story of Nevers and the complexity of her telling of the story in Hiroshima is brought out by the terminology of a number of critics, who suggest that the film describes the "liberation" of the woman from her Nevers past. See, for example, François Mizrachi, "Thèmes surréalistes dans l'oeuvre d'Alain Resnais," *Etudes Cinématypographies* 40/42 (1965).

9. The image of the hand plays an important role in the film, which possibly picks up on its role in the philosophical tradition. For an interesting reading of the juxtaposition of hand images in this scene, see Linda Williams, "Hiroshima and Marienbad: Metaphor and Metonymy," *Screen* 17 (1976); Martin J. Medhurst traces the motif of the hand in the film in "*Hiroshima, Mon Amour*: From Iconography to

Rhetoric," *Quarterly Journal of Speech* 68 (1982). Noel Burch remarks on the significance of what he calls the "flashbacks" in the film not being directly motivated by dialogue in "Qu'est-ce que la Nouvelle Vague?" *Film Quarterly*, winter 1959.

10. It is important to note that the confusion of sight and understanding here also plays a role in the audience's perspective; we do not know, as we watch the first scenes of the bodily fragments of the German soldier, what they refer to or their relation to the body of the Japanese man. Alain Resnais emphasized the lack of knowing—on the part of both audience and character—when he insisted that these fragments were not to be considered "flashbacks": "Je n'aime pas utiliser le 'flash back'—pour moi, *Hiroshima mon amour* est toujours au présent" [I don't like to use the word *flashback*—for me, *Hiroshima mon amour* is always in the present] (Alain Resnais, quoted in Yvonne Baby, "Un entretien avec Alain Resnais," *Le Monde*, 11 May 1966).

11. Many critics describe the relation between the woman's past and present in terms of repetition and forgetting. See, for example, Burch, "Qu'est-ce que la Nouvelle Vague?"; Marcelle Marini, *Territoires du féminin avec Marguerite Duras* (Paris: Editions de Minuit, 1977); and Marie-France Etienne, "L'oubli et la répétition: *Hiroshima mon amour*," *Romanic Review* 78, no. 4 (November 1987). Barbara Freeman provides an interesting analysis that could be read as suggesting that the relation of desire between the Japanese man and the French woman is itself a form of forgetting and of testimony (see "Epitaphs and Epigraphs," in *Arms and the Woman*, ed. H. M. Cooper, A. A. Munich, and S. M. Squier [Chapel Hill: University of North Carolina Press, 1989]).

12. At one point in the dialogue, the woman tells the man:

> She: One day, I'm twenty years old. It's in the cellar. My mother comes and tells me I'm twenty. (*A pause, as if remembering.*) My mother's crying.
> He: You spit in your mother's face?
> She: Yes. (58)

13. A similar kind of refusal of understanding that is also a creative act of listening can perhaps be heard (recognizing the obvious difference between the subjects) in the words of Claude Lanzmann, describing his own film of catastrophe: "It is enough to formulate the question in simplistic terms—Why have the Jews been killed?—for the question to reveal right away its obscenity. There is an absolute obscenity in the very project of understanding. Not to understand was

my iron law during all the eleven years of the production of *Shoah*. I had clung to this refusal of understanding as the only possible ethical, and at the same time the only possible operative, attitude. This blindness was for me the vital condition of creation" (see Claude Lanzmann, "Hier ist kein Warum," in *Au sujet de Shoah: Le film de Claude Lanzmann*, by Bernard Cuau et al. [Paris: Belin, 1990]).

14. It is important to note that the question of comparison, which made this film so controversial—what some people felt was a reductive equation between mass catastrophe and a historically less significant individual loss—has been displaced or rethought by the film. For in the case of traumatic experiences—experiences not of wholly possessed, fully grasped, or completely remembered events but, more complexly, of partially unassimilated or "missed" experiences—one cannot truly speak of comparison in any simple sense. How, indeed, can one compare what is *not* fully mastered or grasped in experience, or what is missed, in two separate situations? Such a linking of experiences is not exactly an analogy or metaphor, which would suggest the identification or equation of experiences, since analogy and metaphor are traditionally understood in terms of what has been or can be phenomenally perceived or made available to cognition; the linking of traumas, or the possibility of communication or encounter through them, demands a different model or a different way of thinking that may not guarantee communication or acceptance but may also allow for an encounter that retains, or does not fully erase, difference.

In a related though somewhat different vein, I take issue with the dialectical readings of the film, for example, that of Godelieve Mercken-Spaas, who suggest that the contradictions between Hiroshima and Nevers are resolved in the final scenes in a kind of sublation (see her "Destruction and Reconstruction in *Hiroshima, mon amour*," *Literature/Film Quarterly* 8 [1980]). Some version of a dialectical reading is quite common in the critical literature; see also, for example, Bernard Pingaud, "Le temps: Dialectique de la mémoire et de l'oubli," in *"Tu n'as rien vu à Hiroshima!" Un grand film Hiroshima mon amour*, by Raymond Ravar et al. (Brussels: Editions de l'Institut de Sociologie, 1962), and John W. Moses, "Vision Denied in *Night and Fog* and *Hiroshima Mon Amour*," *Literature/Film Quarterly* 14 (1987), who uses the term *dialectic* but whose reading actually opens up the text to other possibilities. An explicit attempt at such an opening is to be found in Julia Kristeva, "La maladie de la douleur: Duras," in her *Soleil noir: Mélancolie et dépression* (Paris: Gallimard, 1987), translated as *Black Sun: Depression and Melancholia* (New York: Columbia University Press, 1989). Resnais himself commented on the tendency toward a dialectic in the film, which he suggests nonetheless resists any form of resolution: "De toutes façons, c'est un film qui se souhaiterait dialectique, et où la contradiction est perpétuelle" [In every sense, it is a film that wishes to be dialectical, and where there remains a perpetual contradiction] (see the interview by Michèle Firk in *Lettres françaises*, 14–20 May 1959).

15. One of the ways that the Japanese language in fact opens up new possibilities for the film (even while distancing them from the immediate grasp of many of its viewers) is by using two different verbs for the significant figure of departing in the man's explanation of his and his lover's situation to the old Japanese woman. What is translated in the French text as *quitter* ("Elle va quitter le Japon tout à l'heure. Nous sommes tristes de nous quitter") and in the English text as *to leave* ("She's leaving Japan in a little while. We're sad at having to leave each other") is made up in Japanese of the two verbs *tatsu(ui)*, "to depart," and *wakareru(ui)*, "to separate" (I am grateful to Michiko Shimokobe for providing this information).

This opening up to the man's story is also an opening of the structure of departure seen as a determined narrative. In this respect, the role of chance—in the encounter and, more generally, in the nature of trauma—is significant. Duras comments on the role of *hasard* in her commentary on the film that she was asked to write for Resnais prior to the filming, which is placed in an appendix: "On a tiré de ce jardin comme on aurait tiré d'un autre jardin de Nevers. De tous les autres jardins de Nevers. Seul le hasard a fait que ce soit de celui-di" [They fired from this garden as they might have fired from any other garden in Nevers. From all the other gardens in Nevers. Only chance has decided that it would be from this one. This garden is henceforth marked by the sign of the banality of his death] (126; 87). On the notion of *hasard* in the film and in its making, see Jean Carta and Michel Mesnil, "Un cinéaste stoïcien: Interview d'Alain Resnais," *Esprit*, June 1960; and Jean-Claude Quirin, "Dialogue avec Alain Resnais," *Alethia*, January 1964. On the role of Duras's commentary on the film in relation to the film itself, see Madeleine Borgomano, *L'écriture filmique de Marguerite Duras* (Paris: Editions Albatros, 1985).

16. The French edition places a question mark after the line "It is very late to be lonely," but the intonation in the film, as well as the ver-

sion of the script provided in *"Tu n'as rien vu à Hiroshima!"* does not warrant the question mark, which is undoubtedly a typographical error.

17. On the White House showing of the film, and on its relation to American opinion about the war, see the fascinating account of the film's political significance offered by Richard Klein in *Cigarettes Are Sublime* (Durham, N.C.: Duke University Press, 1993), 172–74. The history of the film in relation to the war is quite interesting: Charles de Gaulle asked that a copy of the film be given to him to show to his anti-Vichy regiment, while the United States Office of War Information perceived the film as provocative to the pro-Vichy French in Casablanca and, in order to avoid conflicts in this area between Americans and French, prohibited the film's being shown there (see Aljean Harmetz, *Round Up the Usual Suspects: The Making of Casablanca—Bogart, Bergman, and World War II* [New York: Hyperion, 1992]).

18. See Klein, *Cigarettes Are Sublime,* 174. In this context it is interesting to note another incursion of the reality of the war—and in particular of what would become the Pacific conflict—into the film. Paul Henreid, who played Lazlo, the resistance-fighter husband of Rick's beloved, was originally an Austrian citizen who had refused to join the National Socialist Actors' Guild of Germany and who became a U.S. citizen after Hitler's annexation of Austria. When offered the part of Lazlo, Henreid at first did not want to take it, but, as he later revealed, he was told by his agent: "You know, Paul, you have one picture a year at RKO. Since the Americans have started interning the Japanese born in America, your situation is very ticklish. You have become by the annexation of Austria a German citizen, so you are an enemy alien. The more you can fortify your position the better" (see Harmetz, *Round Up the Usual Suspects,* 99).

19. The relation between the other events of World War II and the events in Hiroshima are uncannily reflected in the music of the film as well. Henri Colpi tells the remarkable story of the composing of the music for *Hiroshima mon amour,* which was made after Alain Resnais's film on the concentration camps, *Nuit et brouillard:* "Une rencontre surprenante se situe dans la séquence du musée qui n'est pas sans analogie avec l'univers concentrationnaire. Fugitivement surgit un court motif dont les premières mesures répètent presque exactement un thème de *Nuit et Brouillard.* Or le compositeur italien Giovanni Fusco n'avait jamais vu le film sur les camps de mort ni entendu la partition d'Eisler. 'Il n'y a pas lieu de s'étonner, dira-t-il, c'est Resnais qui guide

la main du musicien'" [A surprising encounter occurred in the music sequence, which turns out not to be without analogy to the concentration-camp universe. A short motif surfaces briefly, of which the first measures repeat almost exactly a theme from *Night and Fog*. Now, the Italian composer Giovanni Fusco had never seen the film on the death camps, nor had he heard Eisler's score. "There is no reason to be surprised," he said, "because it is Resnais who guides the musician's hand"] (see Henri Colpi, "Musique d'Hiroshima," *Cahiers du Cinéma* 18 [January 1960]). We might also see an indirect link between the World War II themes of *Hiroshima mon amour* and *Nuit et brouillard* in their respective fates at the Cannes film festival: *Hiroshima mon amour* was banned from the festival on the supposition that it would anger the Americans, while *Nuit et brouillard* had been banned because of a protest by the Germans (on the former event, see *Spécial Resnais Avant-scène du Cinéma*, 1966; on the latter, see Jacques Doniol-Valcroze, "Il n'y a jamais eu de déportation," *France-Observateur*, 12 April 1956).

2o. The story remains complex in its characterization of the "other"; many people objected to the portrayal of the German soldier as sympathetic. On this point Resnais commented, "C'est aussi pour nous laisser sa liberté de jugement au public que nous n'avons pas indiqué que le soldat allemand était anti-nazi, c'était pour nous implicite, mais nous avons refusé de le dire pour ne pas dédouaner trop visiblement l'héroïne, ne pas rendre la sympathie trop facile, ne pas favoriser une identification que le public recherche trop" [It is because we wanted to leave the public free to make its judgment that we didn't indicate that the German soldier was anti-Nazi; it was implicit for us, but we refused to say it in order to clear the name of the heroine too visibly, not to make sympathy toward her too easy, not to foster an identification that the public would find too easy] (see Carta and Mesnil, "Un cinéaste stoïcien").

2 1. On a different understanding of the role of address in the film, see Sharon Willis's excellent chapter on *Hiroshima mon amour* in her *Marguerite Duras: Writing on the Body* (Urbana: University of Illinois Press, 1987). In contrast to the many entirely pessimistic readings that the film received in its original reviews, Jean Aucuy suggested that after this film there would be "no more tragedy without engagement" (see his "Le cinéma et notre temps," *La Nouvelle Critique* 12 [April 1960]). On this point Resnais interestingly remarks in an interview, in response to the question "L'oubli est-il un mal nécessaire?" [Is forget-

ting necessary?]: "Si on n'oublie pas, on ne peut, ni vivre, ni agir. Le problème s'est posé pour moi quand j'ai fait *Nuit et Brouillard*. Il ne s'agissait pas de faire un monument aux morts de plus, mais de penser au présent et au futur. L'oubli doit être construction. Il est nécessaire, sur le plan individuel comme sur le plan collectif. Ce qu'il faut toujours, c'est agir. Le désespoir, c'est l'inaction, le repli sur soi. Le danger, c'est de s'arrêter" [If one doesn't forget, one can neither live nor act. The problem was posed for me when I made *Night and Fog*. It wasn't a matter of making another monument to destruction, but to think of the present and the future. Forgetting must become constructive. It is necessary, on the individual plane just as on the collective plane. What is always necessary, is to act. Despair is inaction, the withdrawal into the self. The danger is to stop moving forward] (see the interview by Sylvain Roumette in *Ciarté* 33 [February 1961], reprinted in *Premier Plan* 18 [17 May 1961]).

22. See the interview with Emmanuelle Riva in Jean-Daniel Roob, *Alain Resnais* (Lyon: La Manufacture, 1986), my translation. Alain Resnais comments on Eiji Okada's inability to speak French in Carta and Mesnil, "Un cinéaste stoïcien." On Eiji Okada, see also Roy Armes, "The Renewal of Time: *Hiroshima Mon Amour*," in his *Cinema of Alain Resnais* (New York: A. S. Barnes, 1968).

23. It had been remarked, for example, in part 2, that the man spoke perfect French and that he learned it to read about the French Revolution, another apparent indication of his assimilation of Western culture, here represented by the French.

24. Resnais strikingly emphasizes the importance, for him, of the voice when he suggests that it was the basis on which he chose the actress for the woman's part: "J'avais vu Emmanuelle Riva plusieurs fois au théâtre, notamment dans *Le Séducteur* de Diego Fabbri et *Espoir* de Bernstein. Comme je désirais une actrice ayant une récitation particulière et que je suis trés sensible aux voix, j'ai été conquis par Riva" [I had seen Emmanuelle Riva several times in the theater, notably in *The Seducer* by Diego Fabbri and *Hope* by Bernstein. As I wanted an actress having a particular way of speaking and as I am very sensitive to voice, I was conquered by Riva] (see the interview by Gilbert Guez in *Cinémonde*, 14 March 1961, reprinted in Resnais, *Premier Plan* 18).

25. The opening of the voice has been anticipated, to some extent, by the ringing of the bells of St. Etienne, which, like the entrances into the cave, are doubled, ringing both during the death scene and later as

the woman "begins to see." The double structure of entering and leaving (or descending into the cellar and ascending out of it) in the
woman's narrative—marked in part by the split between what happens
before and after the slap—indicates that the return to the cellar twice
in the story (allegorically, perhaps) provides the condition of the return
in language with the man; the "event" of the trauma (considered as the
death scene with its bells, and/or the cellar experience) is thus not locatable as a single event, and consequently opens up the possibility of
change.

26. The significance of the exchange that includes the passage on the
flowers, which could be seen as a kind of turning point in the dialogue,
is marked also by the reversal of verbal positions (which is not fully
apparent in the present English translation cited in the text). Immediately after citing the line about the flowers, the woman takes over the
"nothing" previously spoken repeatedly by the man, and the man takes
over her "everything": "Elle: Je n'ai *rien* inventé. / Lui: Tu as *tout*
inventé" [She: I have invented *nothing*. / He: You have invented *everything*]. The woman's speaking of the *rien* not only marks her closeness
to the man's position but can also perhaps be seen as the beginning of
her slowly developing associations that seem to be partly guided by an
association of words *(rien, Nevers, Nièvre)*, an association encouraged
by the man as he begins to draw out her story just at the point when
they have indicated where they were when the bomb dropped ("She: I
had just left Nevers. I was in Paris. In the street. / He: That's a pretty
French word, Nevers" [33]).

27. Michael J. Yavendetti has noted the refusal of the military au-
thorities to allow U.S. citizens to see any of the film footage taken at
Hiroshima, outside of the footage concerning buildings (the footage of
injured people was banned). For this reason, Hersey's book became
particularly important. Yavendetti says: "More vividly than all previous
publications combined, 'Hiroshima' suggested for Americans what a
surprise atomic attack could do to an American city and its inhabitants.
. . . The numerous post-bombing photographs and newsreels of Hiroshima and Nagasaki made them look like any other war devastated city.
Americans could comprehend that one bomb had caused the damage,
but the media did not fully demonstrate that Hiroshima and Nagasaki
were qualitatively different from other kinds of wartime catastrophes"
(see Yavendetti, "John Hersey and the American Conscience: The Reception of 'Hiroshima,'" *Pacific Historical Review* 43 [1974]). On the

discovery of the Hiroshima films that had been impounded by the U.S. government for twenty-five years, see Erik Barnouw, "How a University's Film Branch Released Long-Secret A-Bomb Pic," *Variety*, 5 January 1972.

28. John Hersey, *Hiroshima* (New York: Knopf, 1946), 99, 91-92.

29. It is interesting that Duras emphasizes in her footnote of the Hersey text that she has "applied it to the martyred children," and specifically to pictures that are described in the text as "burned children screaming." Here again (as in the accidental case of the music, and in the story of *Casablanca*) the resonance of this burning with the other catastrophic events of World War II may possibly be felt: just as Resnais had directed a film on the camps, *Nuit et brouillard* (and Duras would write on her husband's returning from the camps in *La Douleur* [1985]—a text in which she incidentally describes their joint discovery of the dropping of the bomb on Hiroshima), Hersey had written (after *Hiroshima*) a well-known book on the ghetto from which many Jews were deported for the gas chambers and crematoria and which would itself go up in flames, the Warsaw Ghetto (*The Wall*, 1950).

CHAPTER 3 TRAUMATIC DEPARTURES

1. *Post-traumatic stress disorder* is the name given by the American Psychiatric Association in the *Diagnostic and Statistical Manual of Mental Disorders*, 3d ed. (1980), to what had previously been called *shell shock*, *combat neurosis*, or *traumatic neurosis*, among other names used at various times in the nineteenth and twentieth centuries. The definitions in the third edition, the revised third edition, and the fourth edition of the *Manual* include the same basic symptoms that Freud described in his later work on trauma, including what he called the "positive symptoms" (flashbacks and hallucinations) and the "negative symptoms" (numbing, amnesia, and avoidance of triggering stimuli). While there are controversies over the definition of PTSD—whether the causative event should be considered to be outside the range of usual human experience; whether PTSD is basically biphasic, that is, consisting of alternating flashbacks and numbing, or has at its core an unalterable numbness that is interrupted by more treatable flashbacks, as Terence Keane has suggested—the basic description of the experience has remained remarkably unchanged over the years both in clinical and theoretical accounts and in survivor stories. In this chapter, which begins with the psychiatric definition and term but focuses on psychoanalytic

texts, I assume a certain continuity between contemporary psychiatry and early psychoanalysis concerning trauma, and I implicitly suggest that rather than focusing only on the current rift between them (in debates between psychiatrists and psychoanalysts over the interpretation of trauma as adult trauma, focused on outer violence, and childhood trauma, associated with inner fantasies), we should look at what each can learn from the other.

2. Trauma theory often divides itself into two basic trends: the focus on trauma as the "shattering" of a previously whole self and the focus on the survival function of trauma as allowing one to get through an overwhelming experience by numbing oneself to it. In the former camp, see, for example, Jonathan Cohen, "Structural Consequences of Psychic Trauma: A New Look at *Beyond the Pleasure Principle*," *International Journal of Psychoanalysis* 61 (1980); Abram Kardiner with Herbert Spiegel, *War Stress and Neurotic Illness*, 2d ed., rev. (New York: Paul B. Hoeber, 1947); and the self-psychological approach expressed in the essays in Richard B. Ulman and Doris Brothers, *The Shattered Self: A Psychoanalytic Study of Trauma* (Hillsdale, N.J.: Analytic Press, 1988). In the latter camp, see Lifton, "Survivor Experience and Traumatic Syndrome"; and Charles Marmar, "The Dynamic Psychotherapy of PTSD" (paper delivered at the conference "Psychological Trauma in Times of War and Peace: Intervention and Treatment," Boston, 7–8 June 1991).

3. Many writers have pointed to the relation between these texts and the events of the wars. The conclusions concerning this relation tend to differ, however. For the most part, Freud's wartime writing is seen as showing an inevitable tendency toward destruction, which is linked directly to what Freud saw around him in Europe. The fact that *Beyond the Pleasure Principle* and *Moses and Monotheism* are simultaneously seen as fantastical or mythical accounts of history is significant; in order to understand either text as simply and directly referential, one must ignore its mythical side, or to put it differently, the referential theory finds itself inscribed in what appears to be a mythical or figurative theory. As we shall see, the understanding of trauma that Freud provides in these texts might provide a way to understand the referential meaning of the texts outside of the historical/mythical opposition.

4. All quotations from *Beyond the Pleasure Principle* are from *SE*, vol. 18.

5. The full impact of this notion of trauma can be understood when we look at it in terms of the inside/outside model of the psyche implied

in the theory of the pleasure principle, which implicitly suggests that what is inside the psyche is a mediation of the outside through desire, repression, and so on. In trauma, there is an incomprehensible outside of the self that has already gone inside without the self's mediation, hence without any relation to the self, and this consequently becomes a threat to any understanding of what a self might be in this context.

6. The relation between intrusion and amnesia reemerges in the recent work on trauma in both psychiatry and neurobiology. See Mark S. Greenberg and Bessel A. van der Kolk, "Retrieval and Integration of Traumatic Memories with the 'Painting Cure,'" in van der Kolk, *Psychological Trauma* (Washington, D.C.: American Psychiatric Press, 1987); and John Krystal, "Animal Models for Posttraumatic Stress Disorder," in *Biological Assessment and Treatment of Post-traumatic Stress Disorder*, ed. Earl L. Giller Jr. (Washington, D.C.: American Psychiatric Press, 1990).

7. Freud actually offers two models that are not clearly differentiated: (1) a model of quantity (the stimulus barrier protects the organism from "too much stimulus" coming from the outside) and (2) a model of time, in the following paragraph, about which he notes, "Our abstract idea of time seems to be wholly derived from the method of working of the system *Pcpt.-Cs.* [Perception-Consciousness]* and to correspond to a perception on its own part of that method of working. This mode of functioning may perhaps constitute another way of providing a shield against stimuli" (28). When he goes on to define trauma in terms of fright or lack of preparedness for anxiety, his emphasis is on time rather than quantity, which ultimately, it could then be argued, marks the difference between the nature of bodily and mental barriers. What seems to be at issue here is the mind-body boundary, marked specifically by the sense organs (the primitive "feelers," which take in limited amounts of quantity in a period of time) and specifically, one might suggest, by the eyes, which are so importantly linked to the nature of the flashback in the dream. It would be interesting to pursue the complexity of the relation between mind and body as it might be rethought through the problem of trauma. On the traditional notion of the stimulus barrier see Sidney S. Furst, "The Stimulus Barrier and the Pathogenicity of Trauma," *International Journal of Psychoanalysis* 59 (1978); Helen K. Gediman, "The Concept of the Stimulus Barrier: Its Review and Reformulation as an Adaptive Ego Function," ibid. 52 (1971); and Henry Krystal, "Trauma and the Stimulus Barrier," *Psy-*

choanalytic Inquiry (1985). On the rethinking of the disruption of the stimulus barrier in terms of time distortion, see Lenore Terr, *Too Scared to Cry: Psychic Trauma in Childhood* (New York: Harper & Row, 1976). The notion of piercing as crucial to trauma and of the problem of extension associated with it are discussed in Laplanche, *Problématiques I.* For an important rethinking of the stimulus barrier in relation to modernity, see Walter Benjamin, "Über einige Motive bei Baudelaire," in his *Gesammelte Schriften*, ed. Rolf Tiedemann and Hermann Schweppenhäuser, 12 bks. in 4 vols. (Frankfurt am Main: Suhrkamp, 1974–89), I.2, published in English as "On Some Motifs in Baudelaire," in Walter Benjamin, *Illuminations*, ed. and with intro. by Hannah Arendt, trans. Harry Zohn (New York: Schocken Books, 1969). One might also wish to consider in this context the problem of pain; see Elaine Scarry's excellent work on this subject in *The Body in Pain: The Making and Unmaking of the World* (New York: Oxford University Press, 1985).

8. Freud's temporal definition of trauma in *Beyond the Pleasure Principle* seems to be an extension of his early understanding of the trauma as being locatable not in one moment alone but in the relation between two moments. What the two models share is the description of the traumatic experience in terms of its temporal unlocatability. The original and striking reading of this two-scene model is to be found in Laplanche, *Life and Death in Psychoanalysis.* On the temporal structure of trauma in Freud, see also Laplanche's "Notes on Afterwardsness," "Traumatisme, traduction, transfert," and *Problématiques I*, 216–19; and Jean-Francois Lyotard, "Emma," in *Nouvelle revue de psychanalyse* 39 (1989).

9. The repetitive dimension of trauma can only be explained by taking its constitutively temporal aspect into account. Present neurobiological accounts of triggers (flashbacks caused by triggering elements in the environment) still run up against the temporal dilemma of repetition when they have to explain how it is that any particular event sets off an alarm that cannot be stopped, hence causing an excessive output of serotonin, which ultimately depletes the system and causes later trigger reactions.

10. See the Introduction.

11. Sam Weber indeed interprets the passage on the origin of the drive as a *fort:* "In short, Freud must *depart* from his attempt to think repetition as a movement of identity—to think, in short, repetition as

such—and instead to think it as departure. . . . What [the drives] repeat . . . is no longer simply the "same"—the Fort! that is Da!—but
rather a *da* that is *fort*" (Weber, *The Legend of Freud* [Minneapolis: University of Minnesota Press, 1982], 139). It is important to note here
that the originary status of the drive in a departure can be understood
not simply as a universalizing move (all drives originating in trauma)
but as a way of indicating once again the unlocatability of any particular traumatic experience: it could always be merely a repetition of an
earlier one.

12. To be precise, Freud says that the child uttered the sound "o-o-
o-o," which he interpreted as *fort*, and the word *da;* in his presentation
he eliminates the sound "a-a-a-a" and immediately assumes its interpretation. Clearly, the movement from sound (or, in the text, letter) to
word to meaning bears some analysis, and it has received some in the
literature on this passage. See, for example, Jacques Derrida, "Spécu-
ler—sur 'Freud,'" in *La carte postale: De Socrate à Freud et au delà* (Paris:
Flammarion, 1980).

13. It is interesting to note in this context that the very introduction
of the *fort-da* example is framed as an apparent "departure" from the
theme of the traumatic neurosis: "Ich mache nun den Vorschlag, das
dunkle and düstere Thema der traumatischen Neurose zu verlassen
und die Arbeitsweise des seelischen Apparates an einer seiner frühig-
sten normalen Betätigungen zu studieren. Ich meine das Kinderspiel"
[At this point I propose to leave the dark and dismal subject of the traumatic neurosis and pass on to examine the method of working employed
by the mental apparatus in one of its earliest *normal* activities—I mean
in children's play]. The game of course is nonetheless determined as a
kind of traumatic play at the end of the next chapter (chapter 3). For
the resonances of *verlassen* ("leaving," "departing") in Freud's writing
on trauma, see above, chapter 1.

14. The vertiginously self-reflexive qualities of the *fort-da* example
have received much attention from literary critics. Most prominently,
Derrida has noted that "its import is perhaps not inscribed in the reg-
ister of the demonstration," and he links the structure of the game, as
speculation, to the writing of the text itself. As remarked above, Sam
Weber has noted the relation between the structure of the death drive
and that of the game (see Derrida, *La carte postale;* and Weber, *The Legend of Freud*).

15. It is not clear in Freud's text whether the second Moses is named

that because of his assimilation to the first or whether there was coincidentally a second leader named Moses who became assimilated to the first, which would suggest an element of accident in the process of assimilation.

16. As in chapter 1, page references following quotations from *Moses and Monotheism* refer, first, to pages from Katherine Jones's translation of Freud, *Moses and Monotheism*, and then to James Strachey's translation in *SE*, vol. 23. Other passages in *Moses and Monotheism* that emphasize the history of the Jews as a history of survival can be found on pp. 116 and 176, respectively.

17. The nature of chosenness thus resonates with the sense of being possessed by one's past that is part of traumatic experience. On the importance of the Mosaic doctrine of chosenness for the Jews, see, for example, pp. 109 and 158.

18. Throughout his work, Freud suggests two models of trauma that are often placed side by side: the model of castration trauma, which is associated with the theory of repression and return of the repressed, as well as with a system of unconscious symbolic meanings (the basis of the dream theory in its usual interpretation); and the model of traumatic neurosis (or, let us say, accident trauma), which is associated with accident victims and war veterans (and, some would argue, with the earlier work on hysteria; see Herman, *Trauma and Recovery*) and emerges within psychoanalytic theory, as it does within human experience, as an interruption of the symbolic system and is linked, not to repression, unconsciousness, and symbolization, but rather to a temporal delay, repetition, and literal return. Freud generally placed his examples of the two kinds of trauma side by side (for example, in *Beyond the Pleasure Principle*, chaps. 2 and 3; and in *Moses and Monotheism*) and admitted, in the *Introductory Lectures on Psychoanalysis* (1916), that he was not sure how to integrate the two: "Traumatic neuroses are not in their essence the same thing as the spontaneous neuroses which we are in the habit of investigating and treating by analysis; nor have we yet succeeded in bringing them in harmony with our views" (*SE*, vol. 16, p. 274).

Jacques Lacan, in seminar 11 of *The Four Fundamental Concepts of Psychoanalysis*, ed. Jacques-Alain Miller, trans. Alan Sheridan (New York: Norton, 1973), published in French as *Le séminaire XI: Les quatres concepts fondamentaux de la psychanalyse* (Paris: Editions de Seuil, 1973), can be seen as attempting to reread the received understanding of repression theory through trauma theory, as do Jonathan Cohen and Warren Kinston in "Repression Theory: A New Look at the Cornerstone," *International Journal of Psychoanalysis* 65 (1983). This task is, I believe, one of the central problems for psychoanalysis today, since, among other things, it allows for an understanding of why trauma theory emerges specifically as an understanding of the nightmare within a larger theory of dreams and since it takes into account the disruptive effects of external realities in relation to larger symbolic and cultural and gendered systems. On Lacan's reading of the traumatic nightmare in Freud see chapter 5 below.

19. On this dynamic see chapter 1 above.

20. This understanding of trauma thus corresponds to the deterministic model of the repetition of violence that constitutes the first interpretation of the traumatic nightmare above. Cynthia Chase discusses the relation between traumatic repetition and models of history in her introduction to *Romanticism*, ed. and intro. by Cynthia Chase, Longman Critical Readers (London: Longman, 1993).

21. That is, described in terms of a possession by the past that is not entirely one's own, trauma already describes the individual experience as something that exceeds itself, that brings within individual experience as its most intense sense of isolation the very breaking of individual knowledge and mastery of events. This notion of trauma also acknowledges that perhaps it is not possible for the witnessing of the trauma to occur within the individual at all, that it may only be in future generations that "cure" or at least witnessing can take place. On the (inter)generational structure of trauma, see Martin S. Bergmann and Milton E. Jucovy, eds., *Generations of the Holocaust* (New York: Columbia University Press, 1982); and Fresco, "Remembering the Unknown."

22. The point is not to define group trauma or historical trauma (or generational trauma) on the basis of an analogy with individual trauma (which is what Freud explicitly claims to be doing), but to understand how historical or generational trauma is in some sense presupposed in the theory of individual trauma, which is what I believe is implicit in Freud's texts. An interesting notion of intergenerational transmission that appears to intersect with the notion of intergenerational trauma is Nicolas Abraham's "Notes on the Phantom," in Nicolas Abraham and Maria Torok, *The Shell and the Kernel*, vol. 1, ed. and trans. Nicholas T. Rand (Chicago: University of Chicago Press, 1991). On more general

questions concerning trauma and history, see Dominick La Capra, *Representing the Holocaust: History, Theory, Trauma* (New York: Cornell University Press, 1994); and on community trauma, see Kai Erikson, "Notes on Trauma and Community," in Caruth, *Trauma: Explorations in Memory*; and Kali Tal, *Worlds of Hurt: Reading the Literatures of Trauma* (Cambridge: Cambridge University Press, 1996).

23. See my reading of *Moses and Monotheism* in relation to departure in chapter 1 above. This is, of course, not to suggest a simple reduction of the psyche to biographical experience but to show how experience and text are linked, in trauma, around what is not known or not fully experienced. Regarding the writing of *Beyond the Pleasure Principle*, as many have noted, Sophie did not die until shortly before Freud had finished writing his text. However, the notion of survival as the survival of one's child seems to permeate the text in a more complicated manner than a simple reference or lack of reference to Freud's life. On this matter see Derrida, *La carte postale;* on the events surrounding the writing of *Beyond the Pleasure Principle* and *Moses and Monotheism,* see Gay, *Freud: A Life for Our Time.*

24. Freud to Ferenczi, 20 March 1924, quoted in Derrida, *La carte postale,* 355; see also Ernest Jones, *The Life and Work of Sigmund Freud,* vol. 3 (New York: Basic Books, 1957), 66. To think about the psychoanalytic tradition in terms of *Moses and Monotheism,* one would want to explore Freud's own thinking of the unconscious force of tradition in terms of the relation between oral and written tradition. See, for example, p. 86.

CHAPTER 4 THE FALLING BODY AND THE IMPACT OF REFERENCE

1. Paul de Man, "The Resistance to Theory," in his *The Resistance to Theory* (Minneapolis: University of Minnesota Press, 1986).

2. De Man says simply "geometry" but is clearly referring to analytical geometry; cf. his description of analytical geometry in his essay "Aesthetic Formalization in Kleist" as "an attempt to articulate the phenomenal particularity of a spatial entity (line or curve) with the formalized computation of number" (*The Rhetoric of Romanticism* [New York: Columbia University Press, 1984], 266), henceforth cited as AFK.

3. For a discussion of the distinction between the law and the concept of gravitation, see Gerd Buchdahl, "Gravity and Intelligibility: Newton to Kant," in *The Methodological Heritage of Newton,* ed. Robert

E. Butts and John W. Davis (Toronto: University of Toronto Press, 1970).

4. See, for example, Paul de Man, "The Rhetoric of Temporality," in *Blindness and Insight: Essays in the Rhetoric of Contemporary Criticism*, 2d ed., rev. (Minneapolis: University of Minnesota Press, 1983), originally published in *Interpretation*, ed. Charles Singleton (Baltimore: Johns Hopkins Press, 1969); and idem, "The Epistemology of Metaphor," in *On Metaphor*, ed. Sheldon Sacks (Chicago: University of Chicago Press, 1978).

5. Paul de Man, "Phenomenality and Materiality in Kant," in *Hermeneutics: Questions and Prospects*, ed. Gary Shapiro and Alan Sica (Amherst: University of Massachusetts Press, 1984), henceforth cited as PMK. The description of critical philosophy as a theory founded on the "independence of knowledge from empirical referents" does not imply that the empirical is irrelevant for Kant but rather that critical philosophy is able to articulate its own transcendental rules for the conditions of possibility of experience as in some sense prior to the knowledge of empirical law.

6. See Kant's *Metaphysical Foundations of Natural Science*, trans. James W. Ellington, in *Immanuel Kant: Philosophy of Material Nature* (Indianapolis: Hackett, 1986). The *Foundations* is an elaborate conceptual system that is meant to be a reformulation of Newtonian law in terms of its combined conceptual presuppositions and material givens, which link it to transcendental philosophy as the latter's "example." Metaphysics is partially empirically determined and is linked on its side to fully empirical laws.

7. Cynthia Chase offers an excellent reading of de Man's essay in relation to aesthetic theory and politics in "Trappings of an Education," in *Responses to Paul de Man's Wartime Journalism*, ed. Werner Hamacher, Neil Hertz, and Thomas Keenan (Lincoln: University of Nebraska Press, 1989); see also Andrzej Warminski's fine essay "Terrible Reading," in the same volume.

8. We may understand this dynamic of autobiography also in terms of de Man's own writing/nonwriting on his past and the ongoing attempts to create autobiographical accounts of it.

9. On the figure of hanging and the appearance of other bodily figures in de Man, see Neil Hertz, "Lurid Figures," in *Reading de Man Reading*, ed. Lindsay Waters and Wlad Godzich (Minneapolis: University of Minnesota Press, 1989); on the function of reference as an

"imperative" in de Man's writing, see Werner Hamacher, "LECTIO: De Man's Imperative," in the same volume.

CHAPTER 5 TRAUMATIC AWAKENINGS

1. Lacan's study of the dream of the burning child constitutes the core of the first section of the seminar, entitled "The Unconscious and Repetition." In this section, chapter 5, entitled "Tuché and Automaton," is in large part consecrated to Lacan's rereading of the dream. Sporadic reference to, and reflections on, the dream can also be found in chapters 3 and 6.

2. Quotations from Freud are from *SE*, vols. 4 and 5.

3. On the relation between the dream of the burning child and Freud's dream of his own father, see Jane Gallop, *Reading Lacan* (Ithaca, N.Y.: Cornell University Press, 1985). It has been suggested that the dream may be Freud's own. On Freud's dreams, see Gay, *Freud: A Life for Our Time*.

4. Quotations in English from Lacan's text are from Jacques Lacan, "Tuché and Automaton," in *The Four Fundamental Concepts of Psychoanalysis*. Quotations in French are from "Tuché et automaton," in *Le séminaire XI*. I have made a slight modification of Sheridan's translation of Lacan's quotations of Freud in order to make them correspond to Strachey's translation of Freud.

5. Freud describes trauma as the response to a sudden or unexpected threat of death that happens too soon to be fully known and is then endlessly repeated in reenactments and nightmares that attempt to relive, but in fact only miss again, the original event.

6. Leonard Shengold provides a reading of the burning as highly symbolic, and as essentially linked to desire, in his fascinating book *"Father, Don't You See I'm Burning?" Reflections on Sex, Narcissism, Symbolism, and Murder: From Everything to Nothing* (New Haven: Yale University Press, 1991). I believe, for my part, that Lacan's text resists an oversymbolic reading, although Lacan does link the figure of burning to desire in chapter 4 of the seminar and in his final comments in chapter 5.

For psychoanalytic readings of nightmares focusing on their unconscious meaning, see Theodor Lidz, "Nightmares and the Combat Neuroses," John Mack, "Toward a Theory of Nightmares," and Melvin R. Lansky, "The Screening Function of Post-Traumatic Nightmares," all in *Essential Papers on Dreams*, ed. Melvin R. Lansky (New York: New

York University Press, 1993). Interestingly, one of the difficulties that interpretations of traumatic nightmares face is the problem of awakening, which, as far as I am aware, is always acknowledged as an important aspect of the traumatic nightmare. A review of different kinds of nightmares, which doesn't focus as much on traumatic nightmares, can be found in Ernest Hartmann, *The Nightmare: The Psychology and Biology of Terrifying Dreams* (New York: Basic Books, 1984). For nonpsychoanalytic approaches to the problem of the traumatic nightmares by clinicians and researchers concerned specifically with trauma, see, for example, Kardiner with Spiegel, *War Stress and Neurotic Illness;* Bessel van der Kolk et al., "Nightmares and Trauma: A Comparison of Nightmares after Combat with Lifelong Nightmares in Veterans," *American Journal of Psychiatry* 141 (1984); and in the context of general issues concerning traumatic imagery, Brett and Ostroff, "Imagery and Posttraumatic Stress Disorder: An Overview."

Lacan's text suggests, I believe, that it would be necessary to rethink the drive through the curious resistance of trauma to symbolism, rather than through a conventional interpretation of the traumatic nightmare in terms of the established concept of repression and the traditional Oedipal theory of received psychoanalysis. One notion that such a rethinking would have to engage would be that of ambivalence, and specifically the possibility of the father's ambivalence toward the child, an interpretation that Freud allows when he suggests that the father may feel some guilt at having left a man who was not up to his tasks to watch over the child. Rather than addressing this ambivalence in terms of the individual father in a father-son antagonism, Freud seems to incorporate it into a larger problem of consciousness as such when he says that it is consciousness itself that does not wish to wake up. For in this case the wish to keep the child alive, which Freud originally reads as the motivation of the dream, indeed becomes secondary to the wish of consciousness to sleep, and may only serve the wish of consciousness, even in the face of the death of a child, to protect its own sleep.

On the inherent relation between burning and the notion of trauma, see Jean Laplanche (writing about Bachelard), "Le traumatisme incitateur," in *Problématiques III, La Sublimation* (Paris: PUF, 1980).

7. See the examples of the accident nightmare in *Beyond the Pleasure Principle* (chap. 2) and the comparison of the trauma of the Jews with that of a train accident survivor in *Moses and Monotheism* (pt. 3, sec. 1, chap. 3). See also my detailed discussion of the train collision in chap-

ter 1 above. The resonances of the burning in the dream with Holocaust burning remain unspoken but suggestive in Lacan's text. On the experiences of nightmare and awakening as they occurred within the experience of the concentration camps, see Terence Des Pres, "Nightmare and Waking," in his *The Survivor: An Anatomy of Life in the Death Camps* (New York: Oxford University Press, 1976).

8. Shoshana Felman evocatively reads Lacan's interpretation of the dream in terms of the "encounter between sleep and waking" in "'Ne vois-tu pas que je brûle?' ou Lacan et la philosophie," in *La folie et la chose littéraire* (Paris: Editions de Seuil, 1978), translated into English as "'Don't You See I'm Burning?' Or Lacan and Philosophy," in *Writing and Madness* (Ithaca: Cornell University Press, 1985), 134–40. It should be noted that the relation between sleeping and waking, analyzed in my essay in terms of father and child, involves another character, the *Wächter*, who has fallen asleep next to the child and remains asleep even when the father awakens. Lacan describes the moment between sleeping and waking also in terms of this split between father and *Wächter* and picks up on this notion of splitting in the third part of "Tuché and Automaton." He thus touches on a dimension of trauma that, in the history of psychiatry and psychoanalysis, goes alongside the temporal understanding of trauma as experiencing too late: the notion of dissociation of the psyche around the event—the splitting off of a "traumatic memory" from the rest of consciousness (and unconsciousness, for that matter). This notion had been developed at length by Pierre Janet, and in contemporary trauma theory there is a certain division around the Freudian understanding of trauma as repetition and reenactment (which, whether acknowledged or not, has a constitutively temporal basis) and dissociation theories, which are often identified with Janet (although Freud also wrote on splitting). (It is interesting that Janet uses the language of sleep and waking to describe the difference between hypnotic and nonhypnotic states in his discussion of dissociation in hysterics; see, for example, "L'amnésie et la dissociation des souvenirs par l'émotion," in his *L'évolution de la mémoire et la notion du temps* [Paris: Cahine, 1928]; this terminology also passes into Freud and Breuer's discussion of hysteria in "On the Psychical Mechanism of Hysterical Phenomena: Preliminary Communication" [1893] [see *SE*, vol. 2].) On Janet and Freud, see Bessel A. van der Kolk and Onno van der Hart, "The Intrusive Past: The Flexibility of Trauma and the Engraving of Memory," in Caruth, *Trauma: Explorations in Memory;* and Ruth

Leys, "Traumatic Cures: Shell Shock, Janet, and the Question of Memory," *Critical Inquiry* 20 (summer 1994). For a fascinating contemporary reading of Holocaust trauma in terms of a dissociative splitting of discourse, see Lawrence L. Langer, *Holocaust Testimonies: The Ruins of Memory* (New Haven: Yale University Press, 1991). It is interesting to note (and may be behind Lacan's own reading) that the *Wächter*—the watchman—in the dream of the burning child resonates with Freud's own general definition of the dream, in *The Interpretation of Dreams*, as the watchman or guardian of sleep, "der Wächter des Schlafens."

9. My reading of this seminar (chapter 5 in *The Four Fundamental Concepts of Psychoanalysis*) can be understood in part as a a reading of Lacan's comments in chapter 3:

> The status of the unconscious, which, as I have shown, is so fragile on the ontic plane, is ethical. In his thirst for truth, Freud says, *Whatever it is, I must go there*, because, somewhere, this unconscious reveals itself. . . . Freud said, *There is the country where I shall take my people.* . . . I am not being impressionistic when I say that Freud's approach here is ethical . . .
>
> Freud shows that he is very well aware how fragile are the veils of the unconscious where this register is concerned, when he opens the last chapter of *The Interpretation of Dreams* with the dream which, of all those that are analysed in the book, is in a category of its own—a dream suspended around the most anguishing mystery, that which links a father to the corpse of his son close by, of his dead son. (33–34)

Slavoj Zizek suggests that the awakening in Lacan's reading of the dream is a precise reversal of the usual understanding of dream as fiction and of awakening as reality: he argues that the awakening of the father in Lacan's reading is an "escape" from the real into ideology. Aside from the difficulty of accepting that awakening to a child's dead corpse could ever be understood as an escape, the force of Lacan's reading, in the way that I understand it, clearly suggests that the encounter with the real cannot simply be located either inside or outside the dream, but has to be located in the moment of the transition between the two, in the movement from one to the other. This is what Lacan precisely calls "the gap that constitutes awakening" (57). See Slavoj Zizek, *The Sublime Object of Ideology* (London: Verso, 1989).

10. One can also understand Freud's description of the death drive in this context in terms of the very specific death described in the dream

of the burning child, the death, that is, of a child. For what Freud defines as the death drive—the originating and repeated attempt by the organism to return to the inanimate, the awakening into life that immediately entails an attempt to return to death—could be seen generally as a sense that death is late, that one in fact dies only *too late*. And what could it mean to die *too late*, except to die *after one's child?*

It is important to note, here, a crucial shift that is not articulated in Freud's text, but is implied by Lacan's reading, from the notion of trauma as a relation to one's own death to the notion of trauma as primarily a relation to another's death. Freud's own shift from *Beyond the Pleasure Principle* to *Moses and Monotheism* may suggest, as I note in chapter 4 above, that the death of the other was always inseparable from his notion of one's "own" death. The peculiar temporality of trauma, and the sense that the past it foists upon one is not one's own, may perhaps from this perspective be understood in terms of a temporality of the other (or the other's potential death). In its emphasis on the potentiality in this temporality, my reading differs from Ellie Ragland's interpretation of the dream of the burning child, and in particular her suggestion that the death drive "is a traumatic knowledge we all possess," as opposed to my suggestion and my understanding that we could all potentially be traumatized, a point that I believe is closer to the paradoxical temporality of the death drive (see Ellie Ragland, "Lacan, the Death Drive, and the Burning Child Dream," in *Death and Representation*, ed. Sarah Webster Goodwin and Elisabeth Bronfen [Baltimore: Johns Hopkins University Press, 1993]).

11. The description of the foundational moment of consciousness as a responsibility toward others in their death (or potential death), as indeed the response to a call from those (potential) deaths, resonates with the ethical thinking of Emmanuel Levinas. Levinas writes, indeed, about an awakening—"éveil à partir de l'autre"—that is linked to a foundational moment also associated with trauma, in "La philosophie et l'éveil." The ethical resonances of the problematics of trauma were first brought to my attention by Jill Robbins, whose brilliant work on Levinas and whose discussions with me about the intersection between the two fields have been invaluable (see esp. "Visage, Figure: Speech and Murder in Levinas' *Totality and Infinity*," in *Critical Encounters: Reference and Responsibility in Deconstructive Writing*, ed. Cathy Caruth and Deborah Esch [New Brunswick, N.J.: Rutgers University Press, 1994], and her forthcoming book, *Ethics and the Literary Instance:*

Reading Levinas. On the specific appearance of the notion of trauma in Levinas, see Elisabeth Weber, *Verfolgung und Trauma: Zu Emmanuel Lévinas' Autrement qu'être ou au-delà de l'essence* [Vienna: Passagen-Verlag, 1990]).

12. This insight would indeed resurface in the history of trauma research, in the ongoing dilemma of "survivor guilt," most notably remarked by Robert Jay Lifton as a paradoxical guilt frequently attending survivor experience: "In all this, self-condemnation strikes us as quite unfair. . . . This guilt seems to subsume the individual victim-survivor rather harshly to the evolutionary function of guilt in rendering us accountable for our relationship to others' physical and psychological existence. This experience of guilt around one's own trauma suggests the moral dimension inherent in all conflict and suffering" (Lifton, *The Broken Connection,* 172).

13. Jacques Derrida suggests, in a reading of *Beyond the Pleasure Principle,* that the passing on of psychoanalysis must be understood through the survival of the father past his children (see Derrida, *La carte postale*). Derrida moves between the notion of trauma and the notion of responsibility in "Passages—du traumatisme à la promesse," in his interview with Elisabeth Weber in *Points de suspension: Entretiens* (Paris: Galilée, 1992). For a more general rethinking of the notion of survival see also Jacques Derrida, "Survivre," in his *Parages* (Paris: Galilée, 1986), published in English as "Living on · Borderlines," trans. James Hulbert, in *Deconstruction and Criticism,* by Harold Bloom et al. (New York: Seabury, 1979); and Jean-François Lyotard, "Survivant," in *Lectures d'enfance* (Paris: Galilée, 1991).

To take up the matter of survival in the seminar fully, one would want to include also a reading of the "knocking dream," with which Lacan introduces his discussion of the dream of the burning child. In a prospectus for her dissertation in the Department of Comparative Literature at Yale University, entitled "Waking Dreams," which includes a proposed chapter on the dream of the burning child, Mary Quaintance discusses the allusion to Macbeth in the knocking dream and points to the text by Thomas de Quincey on this play. I was interested to find (in the context of chapter 3 above, "Traumatic Departures") that de Quincey suggests that the knocking in *Macbeth* signifies, not, as one might expect, the imminence of death, but rather the return to life. The crisis, that is, is the survival. The reflection and association in Lacan's text makes a striking introduction, indirectly, to the problem of survival and the death drive in the dream of the burning child (see Thomas de Quincey, "On the Knocking at the Gate in Macbeth," in *Miscellaneous Essays* [Boston: Ticknor & Fields, 1857]). As Marjorie Garbor has pointed out to me, the *Macbeth* resonances in the knocking dream might be read also in the dream of the burning child through the emphasis on the burning candle.

An exploration of the the literary allusion in the Lacan text might also open onto questions concerning the literary dimension of the passages on the dream in both Freud and Lacan. One might consider, for example, the possible resonance between Freud's description of the child's words in the dream and the words of the child in Goethe's "Erlkönig."

14. On the possibilities for change opened up by the death drive (as a dislocation of the inside-outside opposition) in a feminist context, see Jacqueline Rose, "Where Does the Misery Come From? Psychoanalysis, Feminism, and the Event," in *Feminism and Psychoanalysis*, ed. Richard Feldstein and Judith Roof (Ithaca, N.Y.: Cornell University Press, 1989), reprinted in Jacqueline Rose, *Why War?—Psychoanalysis, Politics, and the Return to Melanie Klein* (Oxford: Blackwell, 1993).

15. When Lacan first introduces the dream of the burning child in chapter 4 of the seminar (in a discussion of the ethical status of the unconscious), he also introduces the child's perspective:

> What is the point, then, of sustaining the theory according to which the dream is the image of a desire with an example in which, in a sort of flamboyant reflection, it is precisely a reality which, incompletely transferred, seems here to be shaking the dreamer from his sleep? Why, if not to suggest a mystery that is simply the world of the beyond, and some secret or other shared by the father and the son who says to him, Father, don't you see I'm burning? What is he burning with, if not with that which we see emerging at other points designated by the Freudian topology, namely the sins of the father, borne by the ghost in the myth of Hamlet, which Freud couples with the myth of Oedipus? . . . [T]his too ideal father is constantly being doubted. (34–35)

16. Elisabeth Roudinesco tells of the death of Lacan's daughter Caroline in *Jacques Lacan: Esquisse d'une vie, histoire d'un système de pensée* (Paris: Fayard, 1993).

17. "What is it that wakes the sleeper? Is it not, *in* the dream, another reality?—the reality that Freud describes thus—*Dass das Kind*

an seinem Bette steht, that the child is near his bed, *ihn am Arme fasst,* takes him by the arm and whispers to him reproachfully, *und ihn vorwurfsvoll zuraunt: Vather, siehst du denn nicht,* Father, don't you see, *dass ich verbrenne,* that I am burning?"

INDEX

LIBRARY OF CONGRESS CATALOGING-IN-PUBLICATION DATA

Caruth, Cathy, 1955–
    Unclaimed experience : trauma, narrative, and history / Cathy
Caruth.
        p.   cm.
    Includes bibliographical references and index.
    ISBN 0-8018-5246-3 (hardcover : alk. paper). — ISBN 0-8018-5247-1
(pbk. : alk. paper)
        1. Literature, Modern—20 century—History and criticism.
2. Psychic trauma in literature.   3. Disasters in literature.
4. Literature and society—History—20th century.   I. Title.
PN771.C338   1996
809'.93353—dc20   95-39927